TALENT MANAGEMENT AGENDA
IN A
POST COVID-19 WORLD

Managing Careers and Career Transitions:
Work, Workforce & Workplace

ADEBAYO AKINLOYE

authorHOUSE

AuthorHouse™
1663 Liberty Drive
Bloomington, IN 47403
www.authorhouse.com
Phone: 833-262-8899

Published by AuthorHouse 11/29/2022

ISBN: 978-1-6655-7592-8 (sc)
ISBN: 978-1-6655-7591-1 (e)

To the life and memories of my mother...
Grace Akinloye. Continue to rest in perfect peace.

CONTENTS

FOREWORD

Through working with global leaders, we have observed how they are being stretched by the accelerating speed of change, disruptive events, and societal expectations about the purpose of business.

And paradoxically, just as leaders feel stretched into new challenges, they also need to stretch and get the best out of their own teams to remain competitive.

Arguably, never has the work of leadership been more challenging; not only do we need to grow a special kind of leadership talent capable of embracing social, economic and political uncertainties but also they themselves need to create a uniqueness to their own culture such that talent across the functions is attracted and wants to stay.

In his new book, Adebayo Akinloye addresses this very issue. Drawing on his extensive knowledge and research, he guides us skilfully through the terrain of growing our talent pool of high-performing individuals. He defines the latter as having proven records of dealing with role complexities plus the potential to assume even more complex or critical roles in the future.

Adebayo rightly deduces that every action aimed at improving the contributions and managing the risks relating to critical organisational roles (both current and foreseeable) can be termed talent management.

What can be a more crucial leadership practice than that of talent management? And what better leadership legacy is there than that of creating a viable leadership pipeline? Adebayo's excellent work signposts business leaders (the custodians of talent) through a valuable and pragmatic set of ideas to the very heart of the matter; maximising talent management as a key enabler of the long-term success of their organisations.

- **Lester Coupland**

Lester recently joined the Saudi Logistics Academy in Riyadh. He has 35 years of global experience in consulting, leadership, and organisational development. He has undertaken client assignments in over 40 countries worldwide and works in English, French and Spanish. As an experienced consultant, facilitator, coach and mentor, his main focus is using leadership development interventions to enable organisational change and successful delivery of strategy. He is the President, London Strategy Centre and visiting Fellow, Cranfield University School of Management.

PREFACE

Workspaces across the world continue to experience changes which have before now been described using the cliché, "the changing world of work." Some of these changes have been attributed to different environmental factors including advancements in technology, workforce demographics, and the generational mix of individuals in the workplace. However, with the experiences of the COVID-19 pandemic in 2020 and the resulting disruptions on a global scale, a new dimension to the changing world of work was triggered. A lot of businesses are yet to recover from the effects of the pandemic; operationally and economically. Beyond the economic implications of this pandemic, there has been an enormous impact on individual careers and transitions. Several employees have lost their jobs while others have ventured into careers they would not have previously considered but for the effects of the pandemic and their options to manage these effects. It could become more challenging to manage careers and career transitions due to varying workforce needs, the growing demands to deal with environmental factors as well as productivity expectations because of COVID-19 disruptions.

Again, COVID-19 prompted businesses to redefine the way they operate, the workspaces they occupy (mostly driven by the opportunity to save costs and align with changing workforce expectations) and the combinations of skills they require to achieve their mission. Many businesses saw the advent of the pandemic as an opportunity to re-engineer job functions by collapsing or combining roles. This provided an expanded job scope for agile and resilient employees who could now assume roles they hitherto would not have occupied.

No doubt, COVID-19 has prompted a lot of reconsiderations not only in the ways we now define "work", "workforce" and "workplace", but also in terms of how businesses operate and where businesses and employees operate from. It is safe to say that COVID-19 pandemic created a significant global crisis that required individuals, organisations, and nations alike to take unusual but necessary steps to cope. At the organisational level, teams working virtually brought a different dimension to leadership and team productivity as well as a shift in skill sets needed to achieve business goals. Similarly, the combination of complementary skills being demanded by employers which is sometimes at variance with individual career preferences and personal goals have become major forces affecting the world of work.

Therefore, as the coronavirus pandemic continues to upend businesses, and careers, organisations and professionals are making frantic attempts to adapt to this new reality while also managing the various career shocks that the pandemic triggered. With the emerging focus on working remotely with distributed teams, connected from their own homes, to increasing agility and speed to market via self-directed, purpose-driven teams; businesses, employees and employers are adjusting to this global trend while considering the implications for general employee wellbeing, balanced work life and overall business goals.

The COVID-19 pandemic has significantly influenced technology adoption in terms of how work is carried out as well as flexibility with regards to where work can be performed. These variations are likely to have long-term effects, as well as a corresponding change in expectations from employers and employees about how, where, and when work is accomplished. Thus, previous conversations about the "future of work" are now our present reality. Accordingly, there is a need for individuals to focus on developing competitive advantage in their careers, including the choices of roles that help them to build compound skills and resilience for future crises.

It is important to note that at the time of drafting this book, several organisations have since pivoted from the initial reactive surprise at the magnitude of the crisis to positioning for potential opportunity. However, the wide-ranging implications of the COVID-19 pandemic on employees' careers and career transitions will continue to affect the world of work for the foreseeable future. Specifically, I expect we will continue to see:

i. Shifting perceptions on how employees and employers view the concepts of work, workforce, and workplace.
ii. Evolving work-place policies such as flexible, remote working and a balanced work life.
iii. Persisting career shifts and career transitions among employees.

Therefore, this second edition of my book aims to capture some of the things we now know about the effects of the pandemic on both individuals and organisations. Particularly, how businesses have been able to deploy ingenious interventions for the purposes of remaining in business, managing their key talents, and ensuring the relevance of every member of their workforce in alignment with the organisation's strategic intents.

- Adebayo Akinloye, Assc. CIPD, MCIPM
Author & Global Talent-succession Professional

CHAPTER ONE

TALENT MANAGEMENT IS NOT A FLUKE

OVERVIEW

Talent management requires deliberate and focused actions. Organisations that neglect these focused actions often end up in a "home-alone" talent crises. It is still surprising that, despite the experiences of the COVID-19 pandemic, a lot of organisations are still not taking proactive steps towards mitigating the devastating consequences of potential talent loss, vacancy risks or succession risks.

In the first edition of my book "Talent Management Agenda in the Post COVID-19 World", I clearly detailed what I considered to be the definitions of "Talent" and "Talent Management". I examined the contextual definition of "talent" from the viewpoint of what the essence of an organisation is in relation to specific individuals who directly help the organisation to achieve its core objectives. Invariably, a "talent" is that individual whose contributions directly help to achieve the core objectives of the organisation or business either now or in the future (or both). **The "talent pool" therefore, consists of a cluster of high-performing individuals with proven**

> Talent management is a proactive risk mitigation process aimed at individuals occupying critical roles and geared towards ensuring continuous sustainability of the business.

records of dealing with role complexities (past and present) and hopefully, the propensity (potential) to assume increasingly complex or critical roles in the future. Consequently, every proactive activity which is required or channeled towards improving the contributions or managing the risks relating to key organisational roles and individuals regarded as "talent" could be termed talent management. Put simply, "talent management" is a proactive risk mitigation process aimed at individuals occupying critical roles and geared towards ensuring continuous sustainability of the business. I believe that the contextual understanding of these terms goes a long way in helping talent custodians and business leaders prioritize deliberate actions when planning and building a viable talent and leadership pipeline for their organisations.

Examining the current reality of the world of work particularly, the triggers that have been generated as a result of COVID-19 events, organisations need to make concerted efforts to pay focused attention on how talents within their organisational structures are managed.

SOME PERSPECTIVES ON COVID-19

The World Health Organisation on March 11, 2020, made an official declaration confirming COVID-19 as a global pandemic. At this stage, a significant number of countries (about 110 countries) had been affected. This infectious disease, according to World Health Organisation had (at the time) already recorded a global spread of 118,000 confirmed cases across different continents and countries, with China becoming the first country with a widespread outbreak. Shortly after the outbreak of the pandemic, the spread was recorded in all the continents of the world with over 177 countries impacted. Unfortunately, a lot of hospitalisations and deaths were also recorded globally. According to the reference made in the first edition of this book, "many nations clamoured for their citizens located across different parts of the world to return to their home countries in order to curtail the spread of the disease, provide focused care and ensure that people were not stranded when they needed critical medical attention. The virus initially had no known treatment or vaccine to curb the spread. As the death toll rose, countries shut their borders, banned travel to other countries and began to issue orders for their citizens to stay at home. There were further restrictions around large gatherings, institutions shut down their physical locations and encouraged online studies. Across several industries, aviation, hospitality, tourism, entertainment, manufacturing, retail and distribution services, there was a total closure of activities as the fear of the pandemic gripped the world. Ordinarily, these developments were enough to alert organisations to focus on enhancing their local talent pipeline development strategies, or for those who didn't have any talent management framework in place, to as a matter of urgency begin the process of establishing one. However, many businesses continued to conduct business as usual, until it was too late

Nevertheless, amid these pandemic events, some employees were able to work remotely from home ("Work-from-Home"), while others due to the nature of their jobs and industries, could not enjoy the benefits of remote work. Consequently, laying off workers, furloughs and reduced work hours became a global pattern to ensure that organisations remained in business or were able to mitigate further economic devastations experienced during the period. From the records, the International Labour Organisation (ILO) estimated that there was a 4.5% reduction in hours in the first quarter of 2020, and a 10.5% (about 305 million jobs) reduction was expected in the second quarter. Accordingly, it was recorded that about 430 million enterprises globally were at risk of disruption due to the ravaging effects of COVID-19. Surely, going by the details revealed with this data, the consequences of COVID-19 disruptions had devastating impacts on people's careers and career transitions. These assertions were further buttressed by the research I personally conducted in 2020, with a total sample of 107 individuals across seven countries. The survey feedback (as depicted in figure 1.1) showed a 21% of the respondents saying that their organisations carried out one form of lay-off exercise or the other during the COVID-19 lockdowns. Details about other findings from the survey will be discussed in subsequent chapters.

Figure 1.1: COVID-19 as a Trigger for Staff Lay-off

MY ORGANISATION CARRIED OUT A STAFF "LAY-OFF" EXERCISE DUE TO COVID-19.

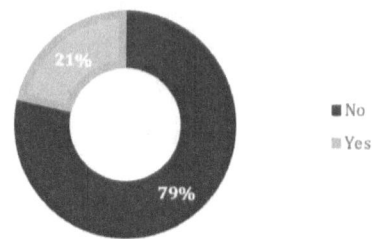

The economic implications of COVID-19 cannot be overemphasized particularly, with the resultant effects of lay-offs and redundancies. Within the first couple of months of the pandemic, we witnessed a collapse of economies and businesses globally which greatly impacted peoples' careers and career decisions.

Without a doubt, the incidents of the coronavirus pandemic were stressful and even traumatic events which required individuals to try to make sense of the new situation and choose appropriate coping actions. The ways in which employees and employers assessed and responded to these events had significant effects in the workplace. I remember watching a program on television in March 2021 when a professor of medicine was asked about the long-term efficacy of COVID-19 vaccines, his response was that no one could really say for sure since we were just one year into the pandemic. It became evident at that time that, while companies were focused on plans to reintegrate employees back into the workplace, the fear of virus infection due to the high rate of transmission made employees skeptical about the safety of their offices. Further uncertainties relating to job security, increase in mental illnesses, and loss of economic independence by various employees created "career shocks" for many workers. Consequently, employees had to find ways to manage these challenges and align their career options accordingly.

EVENTS AND SENSE MAKING
DIMENSIONS TO COVID-19

It could be said that COVID-19 events brought several fluctuations to the world of work. Amongst these fluctuations is the "career shock" situation. According to Akkermans, Seibert, & Mol, (2018, p. 4) a career shock can be defined as, "a disruptive and extraordinary event that is, at least to some degree, caused by factors outside the focal individual's control and that triggers a deliberate thought process concerning one's career." From the definition, two main dimensions are involved i.e., the event and the initial sensemaking of this event. Inevitably, career shocks could trigger some reactions (following individual's thought process) which have potentials to influence certain career decisions and patterns. While organisations find various adaptive ways to deal with the uncertainties and rapidly changing workplace disruptions, employees through their sensemaking process of the event also determine their response strategies. However (according to Akkermans, Seibert, & Mol), depending on the frequency, controllability, intensity, and duration of the event, individuals often respond by taking steps to mitigate the risks and perceived exposures to their careers.

Notably, various work patterns exist, and the occurrences in a pandemic situation such as COVID-19 presents both favourable and unfavourable adaptability options or patterns. The work patterns could be considered along the following dimensions; (a) essential workers: these individuals are required to work onsite and stay at work because the work that they do or the industry they work in requires their physical presence, (b) remote workers: the context of their work and responsibilities mandate or permit flexibility in carrying out their duties without onsite or physical presence, (c) outgoing workers: these set of individuals according to Lindor, (2019), are workers who are about to be laid off or voluntarily leave the organisation due to foreseeable job insecurity, and (d) displaced workers: these refers to those who have already lost their jobs as a result of the pandemic. Each of these worker clusters are faced with peculiar challenges during a pandemic and their coping strategies or responses could vary to meet their career goals and personal obligations. However, depending on the work pattern or circumstances facing employees at the point at which the pandemic occurred, some are positioned advantageously while others deal with the effects from a disadvantaged position. Hence, exploring a totally different career trajectory may be the more effective coping strategy for some individuals. Others might be forced (due to the intensity of the effects and limitations in controlling the circumstances) to put a hold on anything related to embarking on an already planned career or career transition.

In making sense of the pandemic effects on peoples' careers and the career shocks that the effects portend, many individuals have focused on building resilience to take on future career aspirations. Hence, the prevailing circumstances are not considered a disadvantage. By adopting this stance, these individuals have chosen to develop a growth mindset, reconsider and/or reframe their career goals, seek out training and development opportunities, and build strong career networks by leveraging available channels.

The impact of the pandemic is pervasive; from the employee career and job opportunities standpoint, it could cause a progressive disappearance of some roles and an increase in the demand for others. **We experienced a rise in the demand for a technology-driven approach to work execution and service delivery, with a corresponding increase in the demand for employees with the ability to transition into meeting these new world-of-work expectations.** A key challenge with the disappearance of some roles is the consequent loss of status attributed to such roles. We know that work status often correlates with the power privilege, and in most cases, the prestige associated with a specific role or profession. With some vocations being considered essential or non-essential during the pandemic, the societal and individual perceptions of this segmentation could potentially affect the value proposition and status attributed to some vocations in the long run. This may influence individuals to transition into such vocations. Consequently, the attraction rate of such roles could increase. If this happens, potential employers may have to enhance the wages, benefits, or value proposition offered to potential employees. Otherwise, it will become difficult to recruit the right candidates for available positions.

With particular reference to the rapid momentum and adoption of the Work-from-Home arrangement as a major fallout of COVID-19, this development could potentially lead to a perceived loss of status for workers who have enjoyed official perks such as a private office with all the aesthetics, an official vehicle and other benefits associated with their jobs. Therefore, organisations have a critical role to play in supporting the readjustment and reintegration of employees to allow effective recovery and encourage them to take advantage of emerging organisational concepts and practices to build sustainable progressive careers beyond the pandemic.

Furthermore, on the event and sensemaking dimensions of the COVID-19 pandemic, while workers try to make sense of and evolve from the situation, it provides a good opportunity to evaluate and reconsider their current career patterns and figure out how to avert future career shocks. Hence, transitioning into a more secure career or vocation becomes a viable action plan. The disruption which COVID-19 has caused to work, society and the economy has also created a unique opportunity for the workforce to refocus their career interests towards vocations or career patterns that accommodate a balanced work life. Due to the emerging, widespread preference or acceptance of virtual, remote, and flexible working, the responses by various organisations in promoting enabling workplace policies will play a pivotal role in how the world of work is defined. Therefore, viewing this scenario broadly, the experiences and the initial career shocks created by COVID-19 could in the long term, create positive career opportunities and outcomes if properly managed and employees receive the support they need through favourable workplace policies. If changing jobs involves any movement from one employer to another and changing careers means leaving one's established occupation for another, (such as an engineer becoming a musician), then, organisations at various levels would need to evaluate and pay attention to the extent to which the events of COVID-19 have triggered either a job or career change to fit both the career and economic needs of their employees. **I am at this stage not ruling out the possibility that it could become difficult or even unattainable for organisations to meet the emerging aspirations of some of their employees. Effective communication and engagement will be critical to letting employees know the extent**

to which the organisation they work for is willing to support the developmental and career aspirations of its employees. Again, beyond this step, businesses would need to intensify their proactivity towards identifying and managing their talent. The talent review meeting provides an opportunity to demonstrate this leadership commitment. By definition, the talent review process is a proactive process in which business leaders meet (as guided by the organisation's talent management philosophy and cycle) to identify, discuss and proffer collective solutions to the talent and succession needs of their organisation. This process often aims to mitigate potential talent loss, leadership gaps and vacancy risks. The business leaders focus their discussion on the critical roles within their business, the current and potential role-related challenges, as well as recommended actions to proactively address talent demand and supply challenges and reduce any talent loss, leadership, or vacancy risks.

For instance, an employee who is currently an engineer in an engineering company but has discovered his passion for music and is looking forward to building a career as a musician, could find it unrealistic to achieve this aspiration in an engineering firm. Given the misalignment between the aspirations of this individual and the goals of the organisation, it will make business sense to not consider this individual as part of the talent pipeline of the organisation. It may also be a good career decision for the employee who aspires to be a musician to consider transitioning to an environment where this aspiration could be accomplished. This example further illustrates my definition of a talent in the context of a business/ organisation: **a "talent" is that individual whose contributions directly help to achieve the core objectives of the organisation or business either now or in the future (or both).**

> **Talent management is a proactive risk-mitigating process that aims to protect the organisation from talent loss, leadership gaps and vacancy risks.**

Furthermore, the talent review process focuses on a recommended approach towards building the required leadership competencies for the growth of identified successors and high-potentials (HiPos). It also provides a platform to critically examine and understand where talent gaps exist, the required actions to be taken to minimise any impending leadership risks and ensure proper execution of focused development actions which will help in equipping the identified talents to meet business expectations.

TRENDS & IMPLICATIONS

Prior to the COVID-19 pandemic, only a few organisations embraced the concept of 'work from home" as an organisational practice. However, the practice became mainstream during the pandemic lockdowns. Subsequently, several companies began to integrate this practice into their workplace policies and interested employees are now given the opportunity to take advantage of remote work. Alluding to this trend, The Economist in 2020 reported that, "there have been widespread reports about how some companies who might have been reluctant to allow employees to work from home are now discovering the added advantages including adoption of new forms of technology to cater to more flexible work arrangements". According to The Economist, this trend may also challenge the reported 'flexibility stigma' attached to those who take advantage of telecommuting which may in turn, reduce both employee and employer willingness to offer it. It therefore means that there are some positive outcomes which the advent of COVID-19 have triggered in the world of work including, the immersive adoption of the use of technology, necessity for skills upgrade by employees and the positive embrace of flexible or remote work arrangements by employers.

On the contrary, with specific reference to women in careers, some literatures suggests that women encounter conflict between their work and family roles (Mainiero and Sullivan, 2005; White, 1995), and that they are often forced to choose between upward career mobility or family stability, or even having a family at all. During the COVID-19 lockdowns, based on the feedback from the research I conducted (further details provided in the next chapter), it became clear that the conflicts experienced in juggling family and work expectations varied depending on available support. Feedback revealed that, some career women struggled to cope with working from home and home schooling/looking after their kids and many had to quit work eventually because of lack of childcare support. Many experienced burnouts as the lines between work and life became blurred due to remote work.

Again, while considering the implications of the pandemic on people, the opportunity it created for individuals to spend time with family members cannot be overemphasised.

As can be seen in the modern business world, the emerging recreation of what is now considered "work" and "workplace" have provided a novel platform to retain employees and maximize performance and output in line with the organisation's objectives. This has been strengthened by technological advancements which allow employees to work from home or any convenient location provided work is carried out in line with output expectations.

EXPLORING CAREER OPTIONS: AN INTERESTING PHENOMENON

Why do people really want to work or build a career? It is believed that people change careers for several reasons. Some want to do work that they find more meaningful or that makes better use of their skills than their current job. Others might be acting on a long-deferred dream or in pursuit of new interests. And for some individuals, it is somehow less a choice than a necessity. On the issue of individuals wanting to do meaningful jobs, this connects to the concept of "engagement" in organisations. Three key dimensions drive employee engagement; the work an employee does, the mix of workforce an employee interacts with to get work done, and the workplace, which includes the environment where work is carried out.

Figure 1.2: Engagement Dimensions

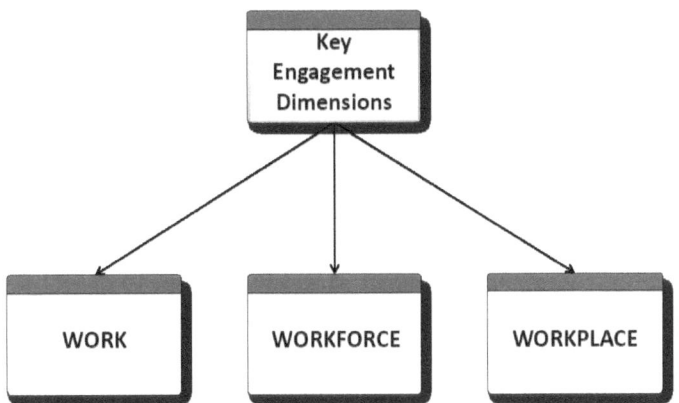

WORK: Employees would desire to do meaningful work that connects with their aspirations and provides them with a clear line of sight between what they are assigned to do and the overall goal(s) of their team/unit/department or the organisation at large. More so, providing individuals with challenging assignments reduces the possibility of monotony and being "out of flow'. From my experience over the years, I have often come across high-paying jobs with incumbents considering quitting. And when asked why they want to quit, responses are often tied to the fact that the job has become more of a routine, and they seek more challenging work. Some would even say that their jobs are so administrative, and they want to engage in more strategic tasks. This development has led to a lot of teams and organisations losing key talents because they failed to pay attention to a key dimension of employee engagement i.e., the kind of work being offered to these individuals. Let me point out that it is important to balance this view. It is not uncommon to find individuals who raise concerns about their jobs being monotonous or not strategic so to speak, however, if such individuals are currently "poor-performing" on the so called administrative or not so strategic role, how would any manager want to assign to them higher or more expanded responsibilities? **It is important to therefore match the identified capabilities of individuals with the proclivity for additional or more strategic responsibilities and transition them accordingly to such roles.** It is not every individual who has the capacity for or even the willingness to take additional responsibility. It then becomes critical to pay attention to the element or composition of the work which is assigned to individuals; capabilities must be seen to match the work complexities assigned to individuals. In organisations where employees do not see this as forthcoming or achievable, attrition within the organisation or regrettable attrition within the talent pool becomes the norm.

> General attrition focuses on the exit of employees across all levels (from top to bottom) within the organisation while <u>regrettable attrition</u> is used specifically to describe total exits from an organisation's talent pool.

When it comes to assigning responsibilities, the importance of assessing the capacity and willingness of individuals to accept higher responsibilities cannot be taken for granted. Although, I discussed the concept of high-potential talent or identifying high-potential talents (HiPos) in detail in the first edition of this book, it is highly relevant to highlight this concept briefly in this edition as well. High potential talents (HiPos) refer to exceptional individuals who possess the required knowledge, skills, abilities and other attributes or whose propensity to develop the knowledge, skills, abilities and others (KSAOs) that are required for the future growth and strategic needs of the organisation is promising (i.e., matching the expected requirements as stipulated by the organisation's talent requirements). HiPos also **demonstrate a high level of proficiency or have the propensity to demonstrate high level of proficiency regarding the expected KSAOs.** The identified talent may not currently possess the knowledge and skills required however, they have a high level of curiosity and inclination to learn. Furthermore, there is a positive alignment of individual and organisational values. High-potential talents are achievers of great results in several challenging projects or assignments. They are also seen to be functional, technical, managerial, and executive leaders, who are dependable in various organisational circumstances.

When it comes to the talent-succession process, the importance of HiPo selection cannot be overemphasised. HiPos are usually "a notch higher" than most employees in the talent or successor pool. Although, they are often identified as potential successors or being groomed for specific future successor roles, you find many of them to have been identified as possible successors to more than one role, including cross-functional roles. They can assume future cross-functional roles because they have built a breadth of functional knowledge across the organisation. In addition to this breadth of functional knowledge, the organisation has also invested time, effort, and resources to develop their leadership skills. This is especially true for HiPos that have been identified as future business leaders: managers, senior managers, general managers, and business executives.

> The "talent-succession process" signifies a combination of activities, policies, procedures, guidelines and actions that enhance the ability of an organisation to deliver on its intended talent and succession management agenda.

WORKFORCE: The diversity and generational mix of individuals which employees must work with in their work environment is also a major factor in driving employee engagement. Most individuals want to be part of a team where they are provided with developmental coaching, opportunities to make mistakes, learn from their mistakes and grow to become better professionals. Where coaching support, opportunities for innovation and risk taking are missing, many employees end up disengaged and perhaps, cease from giving their discretionary effort. Employees want to work with managers who know and understand them and can address their career/ developmental needs in a way that connects with them. When employees see a disconnection between the workforce mix and their personality or preferences, they may become disengaged and consider exiting the company.

WORKPLACE: Employees thrive and can contribute their best when the work environment is conducive. COVID-19 has redefined the conventional perspective of what is considered the workplace. People now work remotely from their homes, across continents and in locations which are totally separated from the regular boundaries of the office locations that characterised the world of work for decades. Many employees have created home offices and the work-from-home induced connectedness with family members has become part of what motivates some employees to do their best. It is becoming increasingly important for organisations to build a culture that provides and supports the flexibility that is now a part of the new world of work. This flexibility will enhance employee engagement and by extension, the talent retention drive within the organisation. More so, key talents now look beyond just the organisational aesthetics which the various organisations project, they examine the culture; if it is supportive of their ideals, the workstyle; if it allows their ability to juggle their aspirations based on the phases they may be in their careers, and perhaps the collaboration mechanism which are inherent within the workplace systems to drive their various career progression and self actualisation.

It does seem that the "workplace powers" have shifted to the employees as they now try to redefine what an ideal work and workplace should look like. Again, compound talents seem to be dictating or influencing the structure of contracts in organisations and, this determines what contract/s they are willing to enter considering their skills which seem to put them at a negotiating advantage with potential employers.

THE PLURAL CAREER DILEMMA

Employees find themselves heading in a new direction after facing career shocks, a layoff or other job loss. In making sense of this situation, employees may be forced to take deliberate steps or actions regarding their career choices and preferences. Their choices or preferences could also be premised upon the attraction offered by workplace policies which provide adequate support for balancing work with family responsibilities and other personal goals. Deciding to take a new job can of course, affect one's life in many ways and should be considered carefully. But making a career change is in most cases a life-altering decision which requires an even greater level of scrutiny before the final step is taken. Policy accommodation and flexibility to support employees during a career transition (particularly, in a pandemic or challenging situation) could provide varying options that might help employees to navigate the situation, respond positively with their coping strategies and progress in their careers.

Individuals go through different phases while building viable careers and each phase is unique. The decisions taken in each of these phases also have far reaching implications for shaping the career trajectory, success or otherwise of the individual's career. At some point, in any of these phases, an individual may consider engaging in multiple professional activities instead of a singular vocation. The lockdown at the height of the COVID-19 pandemic was a major trigger of career reconsiderations for a lot of employees. Individuals who typically worked from 8 a.m. to 5 p.m. suddenly realised they could engage in other ventures without necessarily quitting their regular jobs. Opportunities for "side gigs" became possible for many employees who were now bolstered by remote work options and technology-driven services. For some employees, side gigs are a necessary step towards overcoming the boredom of not being actively engaged. It allows them to challenge themselves professionally, explore other sources of income, activate key interest areas, and turn their passions into revenue-generating sources. For others, it provides the opportunity to become self-employed which offers the flexibility to manage their time, helps resolve key challenges relating to mid-career crisis or perhaps empowers them to take complete ownership of their retirement experience post corporate retirement. Invariably, the career shocks which many employees witnessed because of the events of COVID-19, spurred them on to take unconventional steps towards future-proofing their careers.

As a result, individuals have been influenced to develop "compound skills." These are transferable or complimentary skills that go beyond the functional, core skills which an individual has developed over time, and allow him/her to establish a competitive spiral career path and navigate various career dilemmas or phases. This ability also comes with a growth mindset and open-mindedness of the individuals involved.

Personal Story:

I founded an organisational development and human resources consultancy firm a few years before the advent of COVID-19. As the principal consultant, I was leading a team of consultants and professionals to deliver talent-succession and organisational development solutions to businesses and clients across various sectors and countries in Africa. The revenue generated from this venture was not only very encouraging but also enough to sustain the firm and pay all the required bills. Suddenly, while working at a client's site in another African country, the possibility of a lockdown was announced due to the devastating spread of the coronavirus. The client and I agreed to fast track and wrap up the project while keeping a close watch on the dimensions of the planned lockdown. On returning to Nigeria, to avoid getting stranded by mobility restrictions, the global lockdowns began to take effect across several countries. This led to months of restricted movement which in turn affected businesses including our consulting firm. Many businesses announced layoffs while several collapsed during the period. A lot of our clients were impacted, revenue streams dropped dramatically, and our company was in survival mode. Then, an opportunity to consider regular paid employment was presented to me just as the lockdowns started to ease. Consequently, as a way of quickly recovering from the devastating shocks of the pandemic, I ventured into the opportunity.

This ended up being an interesting career decision which provided added advantages to delve fully into the oil and gas sector while serving as the Group Head of Human Resources for a leading regional organisation.

A key lesson which I wouldn't want anyone to miss here is that career shocks are imminent, and this negates this concept of job security. Hence, career-minded individuals need to understand the mix of complementary skills they need to build as they progress in their career journeys. Some career disruptions may not be predictable however, individuals must understand how to build competitive career spirals to manage and survive any career shock they may be presented with while building viable careers for themselves. This plural career journey provides opportunities to acquire, nurture and put to effective use a pool of complementary skills as career circumstances present themselves hence, matching your skills with role complexities would not pose much of a challenge.

Prior to COVID-19 events, it was not common practice to see a full embrace of flexible or remote work by employers. However, at some point during the pandemic, we saw several organisations adopting this work pattern (either out of compulsion due to changing world of work circumstances or out of necessity) to mitigate any potential loses or disruptions created by the pandemic. Technology created a multiple mix of opportunities for professionals to take on multiple jobs/assignments across regions or continents. This opportunity (or dilemma as some may see it), influenced the flexibility of organisational policies to accommodate this emerging trend as long as conflicts of interest were adequately addressed, and/or no precarious liabilities were inflicted on the organisation. So, depending on the experiences of individuals during the pandemic, the decision to consider a career shift could have been triggered by a rediscovery of their potential or career interests as informed by an adequate understanding of future opportunities or the fear of a loss of opportunities given the events of the pandemic.

Therefore, as it is natural for every professional to continue to seek effective coping strategies as they go through the process of sensemaking, especially during uncertain times, the ways in which the pandemic has triggered career reconsiderations has become a matter of interest. The prevailing culture within the work environment played a major role in shaping how the workforce has coped with the career-related stressors associated with the pandemic. This prevailing internal culture, as well as the support systems provided by employers will greatly influence how individuals react and manage the perceived stressors relating to their careers/career transitions such as job insecurity, challenges of working from home, emergence of new career opportunities, and so on.

Quick Nugget: Guiding Framework on Getting Started with Talent-succession Process

The pathway highlighted in figure 1.3 gives a snapshot of how to get started with your talent-succession process:

Define Talent Goals/Objectives	Identify Critical Roles	Identify Incumbents in Critical Roles	Identify Successors & Readiness Levels	Retention Priority & Risks Identification	Talent Review Meeting	Talent Actions & Development Plan	Talent Benchstrength & Succession Report
This captures specific talent management goals in alignment with the overall business' objectives and strategic talent agenda.	List of Business-wide classification of Roles' Criticality	List of incumbents in Critical Roles.	Agreed Successors' Readiness levels & Development Plan for Action.	Evaluation of key risks associated with specific talents plus their retention priority. The outcomes will produce the Retention Priority/Risk Matrix.	Facilitated session with business leaders to identify, discuss and proffer collective solutions to the talent and succession needs of the business. Consideration for the organisational structure is important.	Consolidation of Talent Actions & Implementation Plans including, the responsibility and tracking indicators.	The Business' Succession & Development Actions Report

Note: For specific details on each of these phases, please check the first edition of this book.

CHAPTER TWO

CAREERS AND CAREER TRANSITIONS

It is a globally accepted premise that the COVID-19 crisis disrupted and affected various aspects of people's lives across the world. The crisis prompted nations to implement several measures, including lockdowns, safety measures, labour/talent mobility restrictions, social distancing, and employment freezes as means of slowing down the ravaging spread and effects of the pandemic. The implications of these measures are far-reaching considering both the immediate and long-term effects on people's careers and career transitions.

Professional careers include "an evolving sequence of work activities and positions that individuals experience over time as well as the associated attitudes, knowledge and skills they develop throughout their life" (El-Sabaa, 2001, p.2) as cited in Akinloye (2010). Navigating careers requires individuals to build relationships between people and across organisations in various environments. A lot of factors affect these relationships which often fluctuate over time. When disruptions occur, the diverse career challenges which confront the workforce relate largely to organisational and environmental contexts. In some instances, many would have to contend with understanding the trend,

> Navigating careers requires individuals to build relationships between people and across organisations in various environments.

fashion out the coping strategies and adapt to the new ways of working. In other extreme situations where layoffs, furloughs, and reduced work hours are involved, the immediate adaptation and coping strategy would be to embark on an alternative career or job opportunities search. Some individuals decide to pursue other passions to cope with life's expectations. Additionally, the events of COVID-19 prompted several businesses and institutions to readapt their operating models to remain in business. This readaptation imposed some discomfort on several employees due to changes in the nature of work, responsibilities and performance expectations without prior capability building and preparation. Many employers did not even deem it necessary to consider the impact of the readaptation on the physical, social, and psychological needs of the workforce. Based on the proposition of the model of **mass career customisation** by Benko & Weisberg, (2007) in implementing a corporate career lattice: there is a need to create "a system that encourages a continuous collaboration between employer and employee to design customised career paths, taking into account both the changing needs of the business and employees' changing lives". This model is an adaptive one which considers career progression while providing employees with career-long options for keeping their work and personal lives in sync, and employers the long-term loyalty of their best and brightest. This model aligns current and future career development options for the employee with current and future requirements of the business in ways that are sustainable for both. Considerably, COVID-19 events could offer employee-centric organisations the opportunity to refocus their workplace support structure to align the present and future needs of the organisation with the challenges facing their employees due to disruptions created by COVID-19.

As COVID-19 pandemic manifests its effects on both employees and organisations at large, the four dimensions relating to employees' careers i.e., pace, workload, location, and role are largely impacted. Therefore, how organisations respond in managing workplace expectations will play a significant role in influencing employees' careers and transitions.

PATTERNS OF WORK

The world of work is largely structured around two main patterns: regular and flexible employment relationships. Regular employment has over the years followed the conventional structure where, employees are expected to follow a fixed schedule while meeting the terms of their employment contract. In most cases this normally required the presence of the employee at the firm's physical location or office. However, the flexible employment relationship allows individuals to use certain discretions in managing when, where, and how the details agreed in the employment contract are achieved or performed. COVID-19 strengthened the notion that some jobs can be carried out from remote locations including homes, and that people can meet virtually thereby, eliminating commuting costs and risks while still achieving their goals.

> The world of work is largely structured around two main patterns: regular and flexible employment relationships.

Depending on the circumstances surrounding the jobs or career needs including family, personal circumstances, environmental factors, and level of professional qualification of various workers or potential workers involved, employees will opt for the most suitable employment patterns available to them at a particular time. Individual career goals are also very important in deciding which pattern to opt for.

On one hand, some workers may prefer to opt for a flexible work arrangement that allows them to spend quality time with family or pursue other personal projects (combining multiple opportunities, gig work). On the other hand, some workers may consider the risk factor associated with flexible work arrangements and opt for a regular employment relationship to mitigate any future disruption risk, or shock, and aid long term planning. Thus, organisations must understand their workforce mix and their preferences, as well as the factors that could/would ignite their attraction to the organisation. Beyond the understanding of these dimensions, organisations also need to figure out the appropriate value proposition that would give them the edge as an employer of choice. This value proposition should also influence their ability to reduce regrettable attrition within their talent pools.

Covid-19 Data:
Data as of June 11, 2022 (as updated by the sources)

Total Global Cases	Total Global Deaths	Total Vaccine Doses Administered
534,887,379	6,308,428	11,545,469,277

Source; Johns Hopkins University website

THE FEAR FACTOR, UNCERTAINTY
AND ORGANISATIONAL SUPPORT

The fear of unemployment has various impacts on the psyche of employees including their mental health. Accordingly, this fear has the tendency to trigger a push for an alternate career shift or transition. So, important organisational concern that has come to the fore is understanding and attending to how the effects of the pandemic have triggered career reconsiderations. Especially when examining some of the personal and psychological disorders that employees have experienced. If this understanding is properly attended to by organisations, it would help in designing and implementing specific career interventions as well as policy directions to support people, the work they do and where they carry out their jobs. These interventions and willingness by the organisation to implement supporting policies will provide the needed leverage for the workforce to navigate the career crisis and enhance employee engagement. Again, depending on the various contexts that each organisation is faced with in their specific environment/industry, or in terms of available resources and the nature of their customers' needs, the interventions might vary with contextual characteristics. As part of the response and reintegration approaches, the organisations' integration of enabling work flexibility and a balanced work life policy could become a welcome development. Therefore, at both the individual and organisational levels, the support structures available to sustain people as they grapple with the frightening challenge of realigning their careers and recovering from the psychological and occupational fallout of the pandemic, could make a significant positive impact.

Furthermore, where the organisation fails to institutionalise the right interventions to manage workplace and career disruptions (such as those caused by COVID-19), employees who experience career shocks with unpredictable outcomes could resort to seeking mitigating actions including, exiting the organisation, or opting for a more stable career pattern. Undoubtedly, COVID-19 created a huge uncertainty in the world of work. It had an immense disruption on work and workforce; many lost their jobs, and for those employees who continued to work, the impacts of the disruptions in terms of work locations, the colleagues they worked with, the type of work they did, and how much they earned in wages cannot be over emphasised.

Therefore, now that there is a perceived (gradual) sense of a return to normalcy which is now regarded as the "new normal", the stakes are higher for both employees and organisations to appropriately determine the best responses and coping strategies to support reintegration within the work environment.

SURVEY ON IMPACT OF COVID-19 ON WORK, WORKFORCE AND WORKPLACE

OBJECTIVE:

In late 2020, while the coronavirus pandemic was ravaging countries around the world, I decided to conduct a survey to further understand its impact on the concepts of work, workforce, and the workplace. I believe, the insights gleaned from the data (as provided by the respondents) will help us effectively guide and deploy appropriate talent and career support interventions which will assist both individuals and organisations in managing careers and career transitions in a post COVID-19 world.

DATA OVERVIEW:

A total of 107 respondents across 11 countries participated in the survey. Demographic details are captured below:

Figure 2.1: Participants' Distribution of the Survey

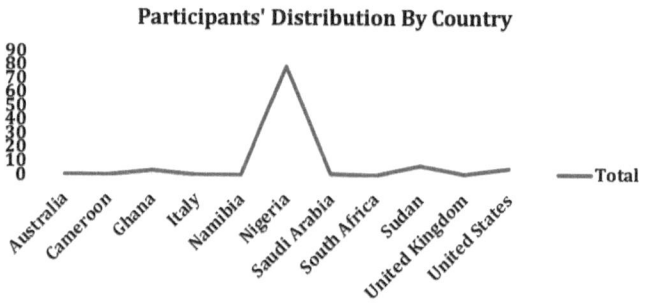

Percentage distribution by country of the respondents are as follows: Australia – 1%, Cameroon – 1%, Ghana – 4%, Italy – 1%, Namibia – 1%, Nigeria – 75%, Saudi Arabia – 2%, South Africa – 1%, Sudan – 7%, UK – 2%, US – 5%. The respondents also cut across various work disciplines: Administrative – 5%, Business Analyst – 1%, Marketing & Sales – 9%, Education & Counselling – 3%, Engineering – 2%, Finance – 10%, Healthcare – 1%, Human Resources – 57%, Insurance – 1%, IT & Service Delivery – 5%, Business Consultancy & Strategy – 4%, and Legal – 2%.

Figure 2.2: Employment Status of Participants

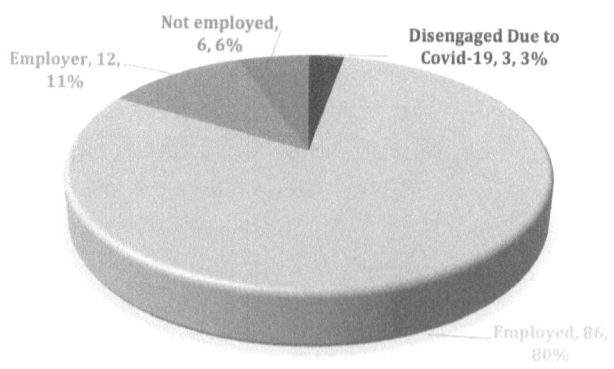

Figure 2.3: Age Distribution of Participants

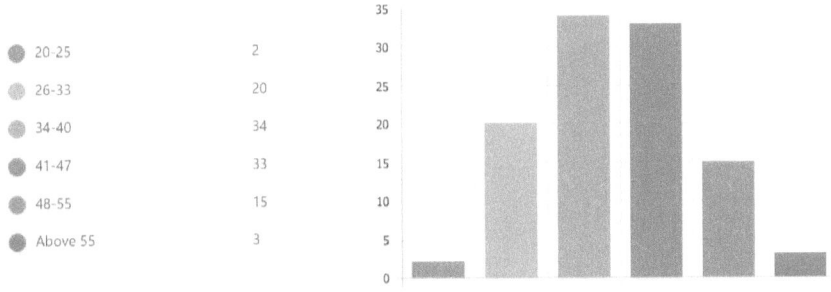

20-25	2	
26-33	20	
34-40	34	
41-47	33	
48-55	15	
Above 55	3	

SUMMARY OF KEY FINDINGS:

The findings are based on the feedback provided by all the respondents who participated in the survey.

Figure 2.4: Impact of Covid-19 on Job Change

DUE TO COVID-19 IMPACT, I AM ACTIVELY LOOKING FOR A JOB CHANGE.

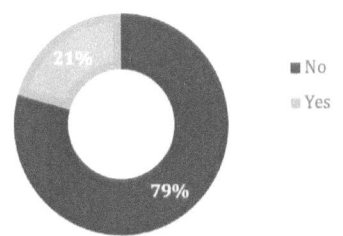

■ No
▨ Yes

Though the pandemic created various uncertainties across business sectors, but for fear of job security, it was not surprising that about 21% of the respondents decided to seek for alternative jobs.

One of the key areas that must be given adequate consideration is the skill sets that employees now require in this "new normal" to deliver effectively in their various roles. 40% of the respondents (as depicted below in figure 2.5) alluded to the fact that the events of the pandemic have triggered a need for re-skilling to maintain relevance in the context of today's world of work.

Figure 2.5: Impact of Covid-19 on Skills Requirement

**COVID-19 HAS AFFECTED THE
SKILL SETS REQUIRED TO
PERFORM MY WORK.**

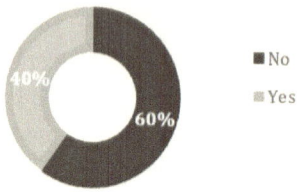

With the career influence data below (figure 2.6), organisations may want to seize this opportunity to put in place a viable career management approach that allows for career discussion, feedback, and alignment of individual career interests with organisational goals.

Figure 2.6: Impact of Covid-19 on Career Discovery

**COVID-19 AIDED ME TO
DISCOVER A TOTALLY
DIFFERENT CAREER PASSION.**

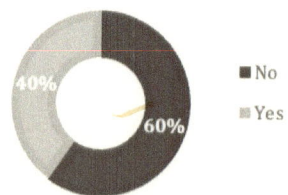

Figure 2.7: Impact of Covid-19 on Career Duality

ALTHOUGH I STILL WORK FOR MY EMPLOYER, BUT I STARTED MY OWN BUSINESS AS A RESULT OF COVID-19.

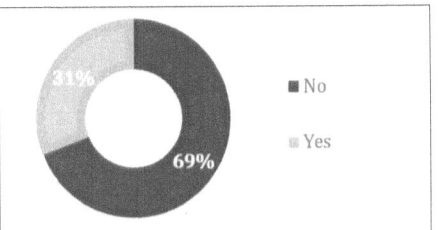

Considering the interesting outcomes of the effectiveness of working from home as reflected in figure 2.8, and the perceived distractions, employers as well as employees might want to rethink how best to achieve the desired business results in the context of new work realities.

Figure 2.8: Effectiveness of Work-from-Home System

MY WORK OR ROLE IS MORE EFFECTIVE BY WORKING FROM HOME.

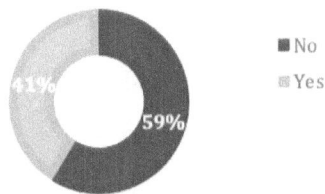

Figure 2.9: Impact of Work-from-Home System

WORKING FROM HOME HAS TOO MUCH DISTRACTIONS.

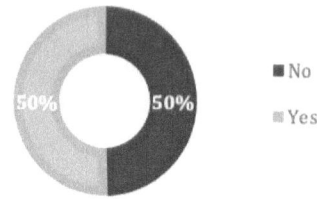

Each organisation will have to assess the effectiveness of "Work-from-Home" in view of their organisational maturity, infrastructural support and performance tracking or management system. This will allow for the alignment of individual employee's contributions to the goals of the business particularly, based on the roles each employee is hired to perform.

> "No doubt, considering the changing world of work as influenced by the advent of the coronavirus, the dynamics of what constitutes a workplace has been significantly altered. Every employee's home is a potential workplace as the concept of working from home becomes the norm in various organisations. While it may be challenging for employers to extend or enforce the organisation's cultural practices in their employees' homes, the flexibility that working from home provides to several employees serves as an attractive value proposition".
>
> *- Extract from the first edition: "Talent Management Agenda in a Post Covid-19 World"*

Figure 2.10: Effectiveness of Virtual Training Support

IN BUILDING THE NEEDED CAPABILITY FOR MY JOB, VIRTUAL TRAINING HAS BEEN VERY EFFECTIVE.

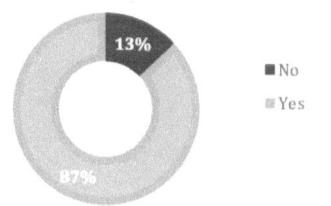

Interestingly, 87% of respondents agreed that virtual training has been effective in bridging the capability and development gaps during the pandemic period. Invariably, technology has become a key enabler in the new world of work.

Figure 2.11: Effect of Covid-19 on performance Management

MEASURING EMPLOYEE'S PERFORMANCE IS A CHALLENGE WITH COVID-19 EXPERIENCE.

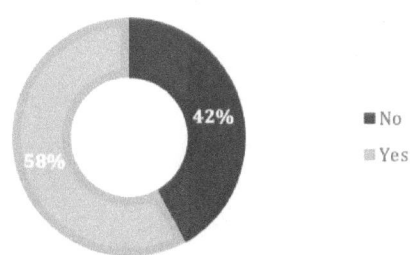

If 42% of the respondents subscribed to the fact that measuring employee's performance posed a challenge during the pandemic, the question that every line manager should ask is, "how do I drive accountability and results in the midst of contending circumstances caused by the pandemic?" It means that strict benchmarks or targets with clear measurements or tracking must be put in place for every individual to ensure maximum productivity or output. This must also be aligned with the appropriate reward system.

Figure 2.12: Covid-19 Lockdown and The Impact on Family

COVID-19 EXPERIENCE HAS POSITIVE IMPACT ON MY FAMILY

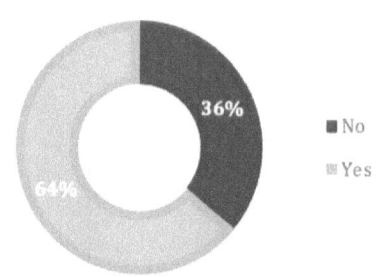

Figure 2.13: Career and Work-from-Home Pattern

I AM WILLING TO RESIGN OR SEEK FOR ALTERNATIVE WORK IF WORKING FROM HOME IS REVERSED BY MY ORGANISATION.

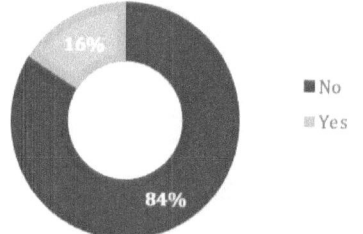

The COVID-19 lockdowns gave many people the opportunity to spend time with family members.

The outcome depicted in figure 2.13 reflects flexibility and openness to different work patterns depending on the prevailing circumstances. However, some employees who seemed to have enjoyed the flexibility of working from home would likely opt out of their organisations if the work-from-home pattern is totally reversed.

Despite the concern expressed by respondents with "Work-from-Home" distractions as reflected in figure 2.9, the contradiction expressed in figure 2.13 is quite fascinating. As I mentioned earlier, it becomes the responsibility of each organisation to ensure the institutionalisation of organisational systems that help in deriving maximum value from each employee regardless of which pattern of work in operation.

As mentioned in the first edition of this book, issues relating to prolonged isolation, concerns for employees with mental illnesses and domestic abuse could make working from home extremely challenging. Employers need to critically reflect on the perceived feeling of isolation and mental health concerns that were triggered by COVID-19 events and devise appropriate support structures to mitigate the effects of the pandemic and aid effective reintegration back into the workplace.

Figure 2.14(a): Fallout from Work-from-Home Pattern

I SUFFERED ISOLATION BY WORKING FROM HOME (COMPARED TO WORKING FROM THE OFFICE).

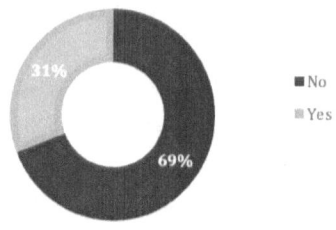

Figure 2.14(b): Fallout from Work-from-Home Pattern

I WORK LONGER HOURS WITH THE CONCEPT OF WORKING FROM HOME.

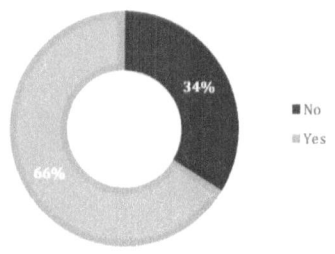

Figure 2.14(c): Fallout from Work-from-Home Pattern

WORKING FROM HOME IS MORE STRESSFUL FOR ME.

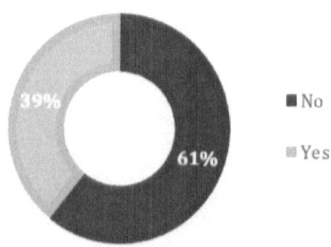

Figure 2.14(d): Fallout from Work-from-Home Pattern

WORKING FROM HOME HAS NEGATIVE
IMPACT ON MY ROLE.

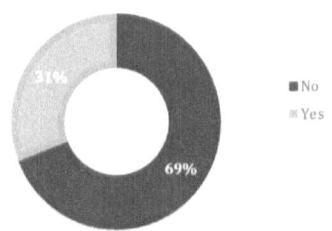

Figure 2.15 (a): Organisation Support and Covid-19

MY ORGANISATION DID NOT
PROVIDE ADEQUATE SUPPORT
STRUCTURE TO ENABLE ME WORK
EFFECTIVELY FROM HOME.

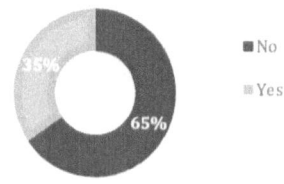

Figure 2.15 (b): Organisation Support and Covid-19

MY ORGANISATION PROACTIVELY
PREPARED ME TO DEAL WITH A
PANDEMIC SUCH AS COVID-19.

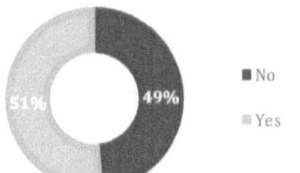

The events of COVID-19 caught most organisations off guard; hence, several organisations were ill equipped to deal with the immediate challenges that were created. Support structures to help employees navigate the unfolding trends is important.

Further findings from the survey showed the outcomes represented below:

Figure 2.16(a): Preference for Home-office
Vs. Formal Office Environment

MY HOME IS A BETTER WORKPLACE
THAN MY USUAL OFFICE.

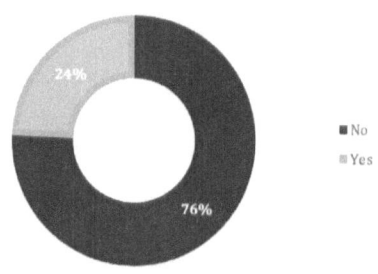

Figure 2.16(b): Preference for Home-office
Vs. Formal Office Environment

I WANT TO RETURN TO THE OFFICE
ENVIRONMENT.

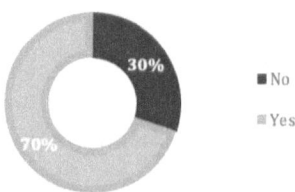

Figure 2.17: Creating Home-office due to Covid-19

A PART OF MY HOME HAS BEEN
CONVERTED TO A WORKSTATION.

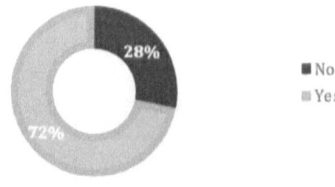

FINAL COMMENT:

Organisations and individuals alike might want to consider some of the critical insights that have been revealed by this survey and adopt a pro-active approach to mitigating any highlighted adverse effects of the pandemic on the workplace. Organisations must also focus on improving interventions and support structures to enhance employee engagement. Any organisation that intends to match these unfolding trends in the "world of work" will have to explore various challenges or risks which both employees and the organisation may be exposed to while initiating coping strategies to match these new realities in alignment with their organisational contexts.

CHAPTER THREE

CREATING FLOW IN A POST-COVID WORLD

Contribution by Paul Leibowitz - Director, Bioss SA

INTRODUCTION

In earlier chapters, various ways in which Covid has impacted 'work' and 'workers' were discussed. These included discussions around economic implications, retrenchments, mental illness, career shock, increased market demands for certain types of roles, as well as the Work from Home (WFH) trend.

Additionally, two key related phenomena have subsequently emerged because of Covid, which warrant discussion, namely the **'Great Resignation'** and **'Quiet Quitting'**.

These two trends and their impact upon talent management and retention have received widespread attention from Academics, Economists, Organisational Psychologists, and the media.

This chapter focusses on the BIOSS theories, methodologies, and tools that organisations can apply and utilise to create the conditions for flow at work despite the **'Great Resignation,'** and **'Quiet Quitting'** phenomena occurring across the globe. The BIOSS approach provides Organisational Psychologists, HR Leaders and Managers, Talent Managers, Line

Managers, and organisations in general with a scientific approach in which to mitigate the talent management and retention risks associated with these phenomena.

Through the course of the chapter, readers will be introduced to the following theoretical constructs, models, and tools:

- Flow
- Matrix of Working Relationships (MWR)
- Complexity and Capability
- Talent and Structural Analytics
- Career Path Appreciation (CPA)
- Modified Career Path Appreciation (MCPA)
- Nature of Work Reviews (NoW)
- Tripod of Work management model

The way in which each of the above contribute to and integrate with one another to create the conditions for Flow will be discussed.

THE GREAT RESIGNATION

"If the 'great resignation' has taught employers anything, it's to not take their workers for granted. Yet many companies risk doing exactly that—whether it's by not paying close enough attention to skilled workers who are at elevated risk of quitting, by failing to support workers who seek personal fulfilment and meaning at work, or by missing opportunities to build the trust that so often leads to positive outcomes at the personal, professional and even societal levels." (PwC's Global Workforce Hopes and Fears Survey, 2022).

The 'Great Resignation' was coined by the Organisational Psychologist Anthony Klotz. Klotz predicted in May 2021 that Covid would lead to a vast number of resignations (Fox, 2022), with statistics having revealed that in USA alone a

> If the 'great resignation' has taught employers anything, it's to not take their workers for granted.

record number of Americans (4.4 million) quit in September 2021. (Jason Noakes & Jeff Landmann, 2021).

This trend is showing no signs of abating, with PwC's Global Workforce Hopes and Fears Survey having reported that one in five workers globally, planned to quit in 2022 (Workforce and Employment, 2022). Their research, which was conducted in March 2022, analysed data gathered from 52,000 workers across 44 countries.

Factors Contributing to the Great Resignation:

PwC's 2022 research highlights five key factors that make up the 'resignation equation'.

Specifically, employees who are 'at risk for leaving' are less likely to:

- find their job fulfilling
- feel they can be their true self at work
- feel fairly rewarded financially
- feel their team cares about them
- feel that their manager listens to them

Whilst all these factors are important and require focus and attention, the key factors, and arguably the most important, that will be unpacked in the context of this chapter are 'job fulfillment', and 'management'. Job fulfillment will be discussed initially, and later in the chapter, we'll focus on 'management' when the Tripod of Work model is presented.

QUIET QUITTING

The origin of the term 'Quiet Quitting' was coined by Mark Boldger in 2009 at a Texas A & M Economics symposium where it was used to describe the 'diminishing ambitions' in Venezuela at the time (Wikipedia, 2022). Others have pointed to its origin beginning in China in response to its authoritarian and rigid work ethic (Foster, 2022).

The trend of 'Quiet Quitting' in China is said to have begun gathering momentum in April 2021 when an online post attacked the old, conservative, and traditional idea that 'work must be your life'. This Chinese lifestyle and social protest movement is known as Tang Ping (Wikipedia, 2022). Additionally, the concept of 'Quiet Quitting, has gained popularity because of a viral Tik Tok video, which was posted in the middle of 2022 (Kudhail, 2022).

So, whilst 'Quiet Quitting' originated prior to Covid, it is evident that the term has gained prominence since we've emerged from the pandemic, and it is often viewed as being the next phase of the 'Great Resignation' (Thapa, 2022). Consequently, there is an implicit connection between 'Quiet Quitting' and the 'Great Resignation'.

What is 'Quiet Quitting'?

The term has been defined in different and sometimes controversial ways.

According to Cesinger (2022) it means "not doing work beyond what you were hired to do and beyond what you're being paid for." Controversially, Lahren (2022) in a tweet described it as follows: "Apparently the younger generation is trying out a new fad called "quiet quitting" in which they put in less effort at work and do only the bare minimum. It's actually called being "LAZY AF!"

On the other hand, well known and respected Organisational Psychologist at Wharton, Adam Grant (2022), counters any notion that 'Quiet Quitting' is about slacking at work.

He maintains: "Quiet quitting" isn't laziness. Doing the bare minimum is a common response to bullshit jobs, abusive bosses, and low pay. When they don't feel cared about, people eventually stop caring. If you want them to go the extra mile, start with meaningful work, respect, and fair pay."

Arianna Huffington in a LinkedIn post (2022) presents an informative perspective on 'Quiet Quitting.'

She states: "Quiet quitting clearly entered our work conversation, but here's why we need to keep it out of our work lives. Quiet quitting isn't just about quitting on a job, it's a step toward quitting on life. Yes, we shouldn't be defined by our work. But at the same time, if work is at least eight hours of our day, are we saying these are hours we're willing to simply go through the motions, with the inevitable boredom that's bound to ensue? Work can give us meaning and purpose. It's part of a thriving life. We should absolutely reject "hustle culture" and burnout (I believe this so strongly I founded a company with that as its mission). But rejecting burnout doesn't mean rejecting the possibility of finding joy in our work, loving our work."

TALENT MANAGEMENT CONSIDERATIONS

In chapter one Akinloye states:

"Examining the current reality regarding the world of work, particularly the triggers that have been generated as a result of COVID-19 events, organisations now need more deliberate efforts to pay focused attention to how talents within their organisational structures are managed."

Following on from this, **it is clear that both the 'Great Resignation' and 'Quiet Quitting' pose serious threats to organisations from a 'talent' perspective.** Some of these threats include:

- Talent attrition i.e., losing skilled employees to competitors or new passions
- Added pressure on the employees who choose to stay
- Employee disengagement contributing to a reduction in productivity, commitment, and morale
- A reduced level of innovation, ideas generation and ingenuity
- Creating a culture of uncertainty
- Talent pipelining, manpower and succession planning uncertainty
- Having the 'right' talent to implement the organisation's strategic intent
- Having the 'right' talent to ensure continued competitiveness, sustainability, and relevance

In light of these threats, organisations need to find ways to mitigate the negative effects and risks associated with the 'Great Resignation' and 'Quiet Quitting'.

Available literature (Powell, 2021); (Blog: 6 Strategies to Combat the Great Resignation); (Breitling, F; Dhar, J, Ebeling, R & Lovich, D; 2021); (Shelton, 2022) points to a number of solutions that organisations can implement to achieve this, namely:

- Incentivising loyalty
- Elevating and articulating organisational purpose
- Prioritising culture and connection
- Embracing flexibility, hybrid, and remote work
- Encouraging open communication
- Providing opportunities for employees to develop and grow
- Focusing on employee experience
- Understanding how employees' needs, priorities and expectations have changed
- Addressing burnout
- Enhancing workplace wellbeing
- Promoting a healthy work-life balance
- Avoiding overworking teams
- Listening to teams
- Not buying into the hustle culture mentality
- Ensuring employees feel valued
- Utilising interim talent.

Each solution above has a role to play and should be considered by organisations.

However, for the purposes of this chapter, **two unique** approaches are discussed. The first focuses on the BIOSS' methodology of analysing both structure and people, in order to determine and create the conditions for employees to experience flow at work. The second, related approach, focuses on utilising BIOSS' management model called the Tripod of Work, as a means of enhancing the relationships between managers and employees, or leaders and team-members. The former approach essentially addresses the need to enhance job / work fulfilment. The logic is that the more employees experience flow at work, the more likely they are to feel fulfilled and less likely to resign and / or quietly quit.

> The more employees experience flow at work, the more likely they are to feel fulfilled and less likely to resign and / or quietly quit.

As stated by Holt (2022), a Clinical Psychologist and co-founder and Director of Working Mindset: "the key to preventing employees getting in this state is to ensure that people are engaged in their work and that work provides purpose and meaning for people. Employees need to feel part of a bigger picture, to have autonomy and control, and to feel psychologically safe – all the things that we know make a good day at work,".

What constitutes job fulfillment varies from one employee to the next, however there are some broadly agreed factors that apply. These include:

- Being able to see how one's work contributes to the organisation's overall purpose
- Having the right work environment and leadership model
- Upskilling, autonomy, and empowerment
- The ability to be one's authentic self
- Relationships, or a sense of belonging and having a connection to others
- Growth opportunities
- Healthy workplace culture
- Recognition
- Consistent engagement
- Values alignment

The latter approach (i.e., using the Tripod of Work management model) addresses the need to provide employees with purpose and meaning, as well as autonomy and control within the context of their working relationships. Additionally, the application of the Tripod of Work directly seeks to enhance the working relationships between employees and managers. This is important as research (Zenger, J and Folkman, J; 2022) indicates that 'quiet quitting' in particular is usually 'less about an employee's willingness to work harder, and more about a manager's ability to build a relationship with their employees.'

BIOSS Methodologies for Mitigating the Talent Risks of the 'Great Resignation' and 'Quiet Quitting'

THE FLOW STATE

It is widely agreed that 'happy' employees are 'productive' employees, and that people seek happiness at work because we spend a significant portion of our lives working, and it's a source of meaning and purpose.

To be happy at work requires employees to be truly engaged and absorbed with what they do. Hungarian Psychologist Mihaly Csikszentmihalyi (1975) was the first to research this mental state of true engagement, which he called the Flow State. Csikszentmihalyi's interest in the Flow State was influenced and stimulated by his fascination with artists who would essentially get lost in their work. Artists, especially painters, got so immersed in their work that they would disregard their need for food, water and even sleep.

Csikszentmihalyi (1975) defined **Flow** as follows:

> "'Flow is the positive experience created when challenges are congruent with the skills/capability of the individual'.

> Gillian Stamp, who is the founder of BIOSS, describes flow as:

> "A state in which people are so involved in an activity that nothing else seems to matter; the experience is so enjoyable that people will do it for the sheer sake of doing it."

Csikszentmihalyi highlighted a number of conditions that need to be present in order for the flow state to be entered (Souders, B; 2019). He clustered these into nine dimensions namely:

1. presence of clear goals;
2. availability of immediate feedback;
3. match of challenges with adequate personal skills;
4. merging of action and awareness;
5. focused attention and concentration on the task at hand;
6. perception of control over the situation;
7. loss of self-consciousness;
8. absorption so intense that it alters the sense of time; and
9. intrinsic motivation and autonomous initiative (Csíkszentmihályi, 1990).

When consultants in the BIOSS global network refer to the concept of Flow, they, whilst being aware of the multifaceted nature of Flow, focus on it as being primarily the match between individual **capability** and the **demands of a role**.

The importance of the match between challenge and skill is emphasised by Souders (2019) who states: "the key to success here is setting challenges that are neither too demanding nor too simple for one's abilities."

Similarly, Csíkszentmihályi (1990) stated that Flow is about: "a constant balancing act between anxiety, where the difficulty is too high for the person's skill, and boredom, where the difficulty is too low".

Further, a study by Tozman, Zhang, & Vollmeyer (2016) reported that when peoples' skills match the challenges they face, they perform at their best, but when their skills exceed the challenges people become bored. Additionally, when the challenge is too high, stress is experienced and one's body releases large amounts of cortisol in response.

To understand the operationalisation of the construct of Flow within the BIOSS context, it is important to understand the central of the work BIOSS does. Gillian Stamp describes it in the following way:

"For 40 years, BIOSS (Brunel Institute of Organisation and Social Studies) has been working with people and organisations in different sectors across the world, as they make decisions in the face of uncertainty. These are the decisions where the 'facts' are not available and are not going to be available. In those times, we do not, and cannot, know what to do and so have to use our judgement."

Following on from this, Stamp describes Flow in the BIOSS context: **"the deceptively simple idea that lies behind our work is that people feel best able to use their judgement when the challenges offered by their environment are matched by their capability to engage with them."**

Simply put, **Flow** is the dynamic relationship between challenge (work complexity) and capability.

In order to understand the mechanics of this relationship, it is critical to unpack what is understood by the constructs of 'challenge (work complexity)' and 'capability'.

CHALLENGE / WORK COMPLEXITY

Engaging with complexity is a fundamental part of the BIOSS perspective and the challenge of complexity is everywhere:

- in the environment within which an organisation operates,
- in the work of the organisation itself,
- in the decisions individuals within the organisation must make during their working day.

BIOSS' approach to understanding complexity is facilitated by the Matrix of Working Relationships (MWR) model.

The model identifies **seven themes of work**, differentiated on the basis of complexity and time-span of decision-making. No theme of work is more important than the other, and each has a specific value-add that provides a unique contribution to the flow of work within organisations. Every organisation, and in particular larger organisations, require work to be carried out effectively in each of these themes, though not all themes are necessarily present in every organisation.

The MWR model can be viewed as a whole or divided into three parts:

1. **The Operational Matrix**

   - Where the themes of <u>Quality</u>, <u>Service</u> and <u>Practice</u> focus on adding value for the present, and results become apparent within a time horizon of less than two years.

2. **The Organisational Matrix**

   - Where the themes of <u>Strategic Development</u> and <u>Strategic Intent</u> focus on longer-term objectives of the organisation, and time horizons can stretch up to ten years.

3. **The Strategic Matrix**

   - Where the themes of <u>Corporate Citizenship</u> and <u>Corporate Prescience</u> focus on long-term strategic functioning and sustained viability of organisations for future generations, with time frames exceeding 25 years.

The MWR model can be seen below:

Figure 3.1: Matrix of Working Relationships (MWR) model

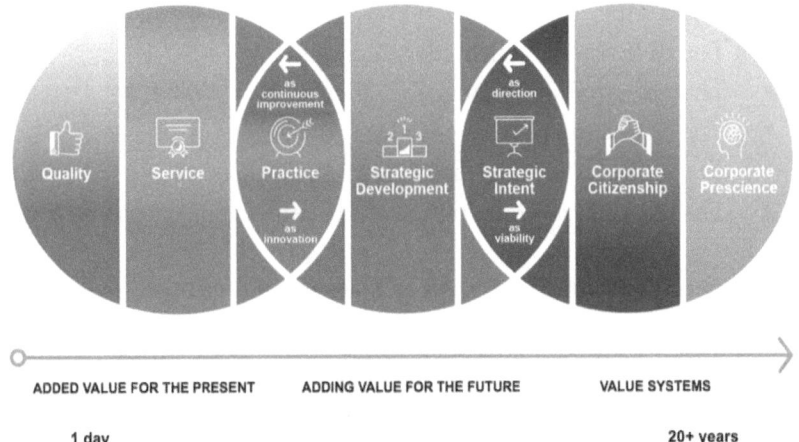

Figure 3.2: Themes of Work

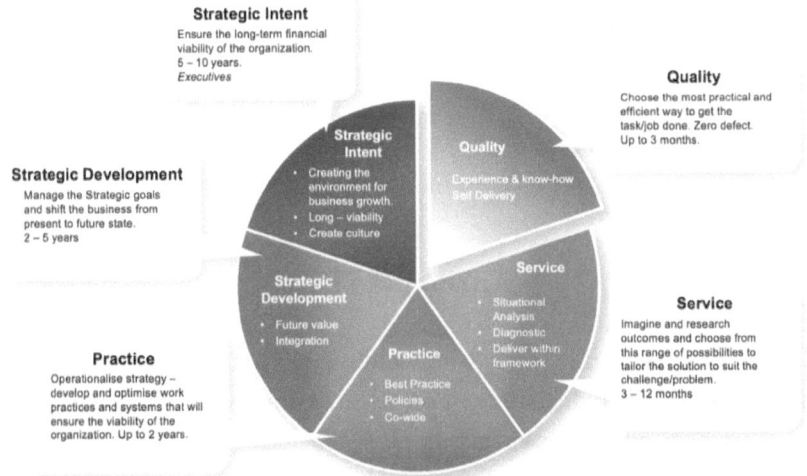

As one moves from the Operational Matrix through to the Strategic Matrix so work becomes more complex in nature. In the BIOSS context, work therefore becomes more complex as:

- Uncertainty increases
- The diversity of stakeholders increases
- The time span of consequence increases
- The environment becomes more abstract
- The variables to juggle become more diverse
- The use of judgment and insight becomes more predominant

Side Note on Time Span of Discretion (consequence)

Time Span of Discretion

Half a century ago, while advising a UK Metals company, Elliott Jaques noticed that workers at different levels of the company had very different time horizons.

Line workers focused on tasks that could be completed in a single shift, while managers devoted their energies to tasks requiring six months or more to complete. Meanwhile, their CEO was pursuing goals realizable only over the span of several years.

After several decades of empirical study, Jaques concluded that just as humans differ in intelligence, we differ in our ability to handle time-dependent complexity.

We all have a natural time horizon we are comfortable with, what Jaques called "Time span of discretion," or the length of the longest task an individual can successfully and comfortably undertake.

Jaques also noted that effective organisations were comprised of workers of differing time spans of discretion, each working at a level of natural comfort. If a worker's job was beyond their natural time span of discretion, they would fail. If it was less, they would be insufficiently challenged, and thus unhappy.

CAPABILITY

Capability refers to the way in which individuals **exercise judgement and discretion to make decisions** in response to contextual demands. Thus, the individual **generates meaning** and can **make decisions** despite the presence of various degrees of **complexity.**

The **exercise of discretion** refers to:

- the judgement we make when we do not and cannot know what to do (where knowledge and experience no longer suffice)
- there is uncertainty and therefore risk involved
- we can't be entirely sure about the outcomes upfront

Other terms that can be used to describe 'capability' are:

- Judgement
- Gut-feel
- Strategic intuition
- Insight
- Wisdom
- Discretion

Elliott Jaques described 'judgement' as:

"a sphere of psychological activity, which, although extremely familiar, remains conceptually ill defined. There is no satisfactory, commonly employed, and accepted language for it. We speak about judgement, intuition, nous, know-how, common sense, hunch…we cannot put into words what it is that we are taking into account in doing what we are doing, and in that sense, we do not know that what we are doing will get us where we want to go, will achieve the result we want to achieve. We judge that it will, we think it will, but we are not sure, and only time will tell."

It is important to note that **capability is fluid in nature, and that people's capability grows and matures over time, though this growth in capability may occur at different rates for different people.** BIOSS makes use of what is called the **Growth Curve** to understand the development of capability over time.

An example of a growth curve is seen below:

Figure 3.3: Growth Curve Example

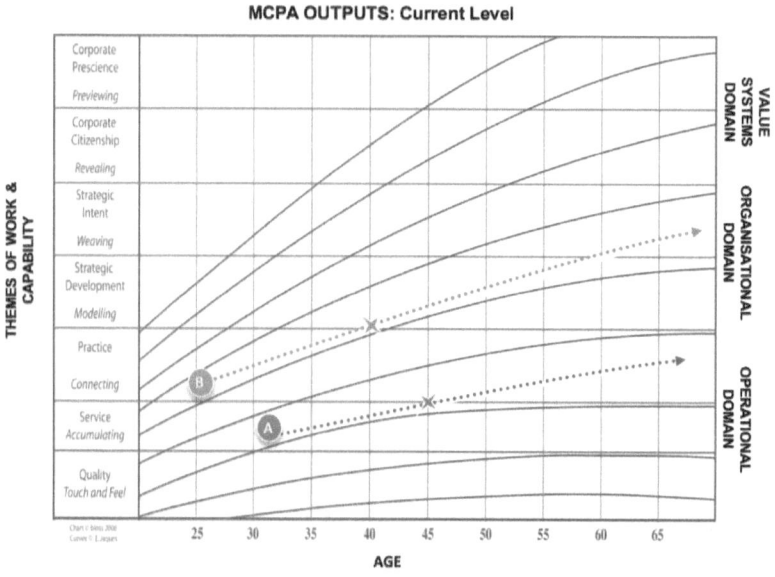

Chart © Bioss, Growth Curves © E. Jaques

The chart above reflects the following

- Chart with person A and person B
- Person A is a mode (future potential) Mid Practice (Theme 3)
- Person B is a mode (future potential) Mid Strategic Intent (Theme 5)
- Transition points shown on chart.

Two Sides of the Coin

When operationalising the construct of Flow we therefore need to consider two sides of the coin:

- The complexity of the work being done, and
- The capability of people to do this work

A match between these two sides of the coin creates a state of 'Flow'.

The two Flow diagrams below highlight the dynamic relationship between **challenge** and **capability**.

Figures 3.4 and 3.5: Flow Diagrams

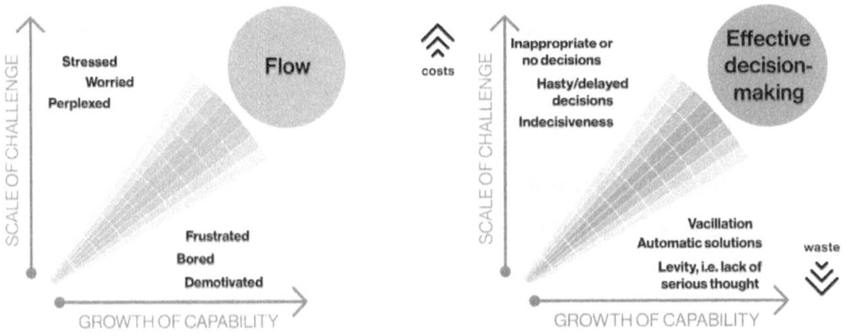

Outcomes: Flow, Underutilisation and Overstretched

As we know when employees' 'capability' is commensurate with the 'complexity' requirements of their roles they are likely to experience Flow. The experience of Flow is associated with the following enhanced individual and organisational outcomes:

- Engagement
- Energy
- Information processing
- Decision-making
- Creativity, learning, and lateral thinking
- Motivation, commitment, and efficiency
- Talent retention, productivity, and profitability

Additionally, one of the most significant benefits of being in Flow is that it leads to improved performance. According to Steven Kotler (2014) the 10, 000 hours that are required to master any skill, as per Malcolm Gladwell's claim, can be cut in half by being in a state of Flow.

Ultimately, all of these positive outcomes lead to employees experiencing greater fulfilment at work.

However, what happens when employees are either Underutilised or Overstretched?

If an employee's capability exceeds the complexity requirements of the role, he / she is likely to feel underutilised or underwhelmed. Consequently, the employee is likely to:

- Feel bored or frustrated
- Try to show their boss up
- Feel anxious and / or aggressive
- May interfere with others
- Feel generally demotivated
- Make poor, automatic decisions or vacillate when making decisions

On the other hand, if the complexity of work exceeds the employee's capability, then he / she is likely to have been overpromoted and left feeling overwhelmed and / or overstretched. Consequently, the employee is likely to:

- Feel perplexed or anxious
- Use positional power
- Go into crisis management
- Withhold information
- Become depressed
- Pull the theme of work down of the job role he / she holds
- Make inappropriate decisions
- Be hasty or delayed when making decisions
- Be indecisive

Consequently, employees who are either feeling underutilised or overstretched in their roles are more likely to be susceptible to the appeal of the 'Great Resignations' and 'Quiet Quitting'.

DETERMINING WORK COMPLEXITY
AND INDIVIDUAL CAPABILITY

To determine whether an employee is likely to be in Flow requires both an evaluation of work complexity, as well as an assessment of individual capability (i.e, analysing both sides of the coin).

BIOSS employs a scientific and unique approach to determining both.

From a 'work complexity' perspective, BIOSS applies a sophisticated organisational design methodology called a Nature of Work (NoW) Review. The NoW Review produces multiple outputs including the:

- Alignment of structure to strategy
- Identification of structural wastage, cost, and ineffectiveness
- Diagnosis of structural deficits, such as overcrowding, overlap, or gaps in the structure
- Understanding of organisational and job complexity in terms of Themes of Work
- Matching of individual capability to the work complexity of their jobs
- Ultimate improvement of organisational and people effectiveness and performance

Whilst the NoW Review provides organisations with a comprehensive structural analysis, it importantly aligns every job role to a required and / or actual Theme of Work. This implies that post the analysis, the precise complexity requirements of every job role in the structure are evident, as are the 'capability' requirements to experience Flow in each role. In terms of work complexity an organisational output could look like this below (Figure 3.6):

Figure 3.6: Finance Department Organisational Chart Example

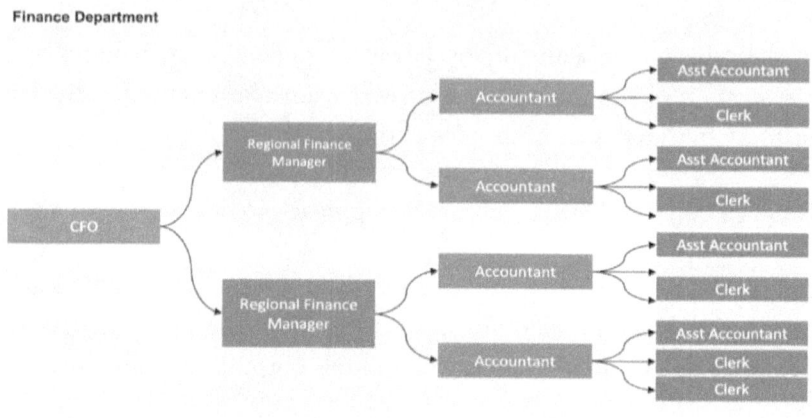

Figure 3.7: Finance Department including Required Themes of Work per Role

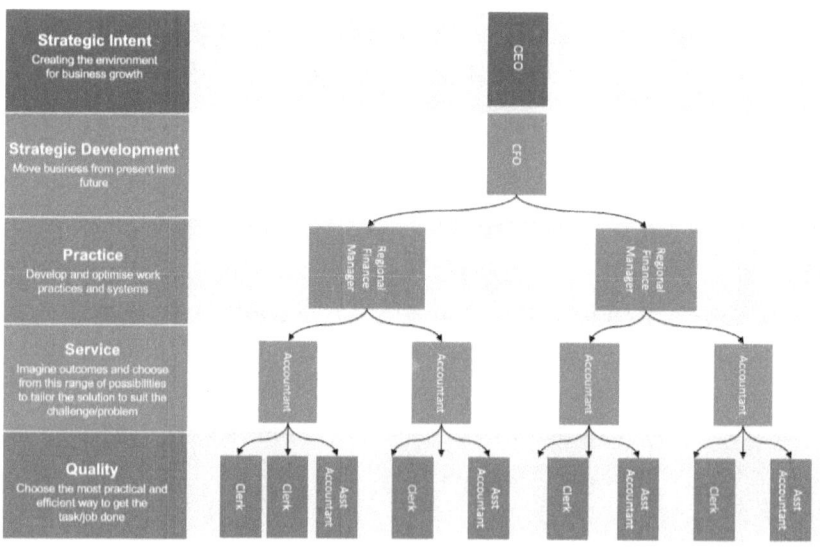

Figure 3.7 shows each job role in the finance department, as well as their relevant Themes of Work e.g. The CEO is aligned to the ***Strategic Intent*** Theme of Work, the CFO the ***Strategic Development*** Theme, and the Regional Finance Manager roles the ***Practice*** Theme.

To determine the 'capability' component of the equation, BIOSS makes use of a number of capability assessments, which comprise what is referred to as the 'capability spectrum'. The capability spectrum includes the following assessments:

- Career Path Appreciation (CPA)
- Modified Career Path Appreciation (MCPA)
- MCPA-SCAN
- IRIS

Whilst these capability assessments differ slightly in terms of process and the organisational level at which they are utilised, they all determine both **Current level of Capability (CLC)** and **Future Potential (referred to as Mode)**. However, the CPA and MCPA, which are senior level capability assessments, also determine **Transition Ages** i.e., the age at which an individual transitions from one theme of work to the next, which provides an indication of talent readiness.

Figure 3.8: Capability Results Example

	Name	Age	Current Level of Capability (CLC)	Mode / Future Potential	Transition Age
1	Sally Sample	39	Low Mid Service	High Service	N/A
2	Bob Sample	36	Mid Practice	High Strategic Development	44
3	Tracy Sample	30	Mid Service	High Practice	35
4	John Sample	49	High Practice	Mid Strategic Development	N/A

Talent and Structural Analytics

Once an organisation has both 'capability' and 'complexity' data, various talent and structural analytics can be generated, including Organisational Maps, as well as Capability and Flow Balance Sheets.

Figure 3.9: Organisational Map

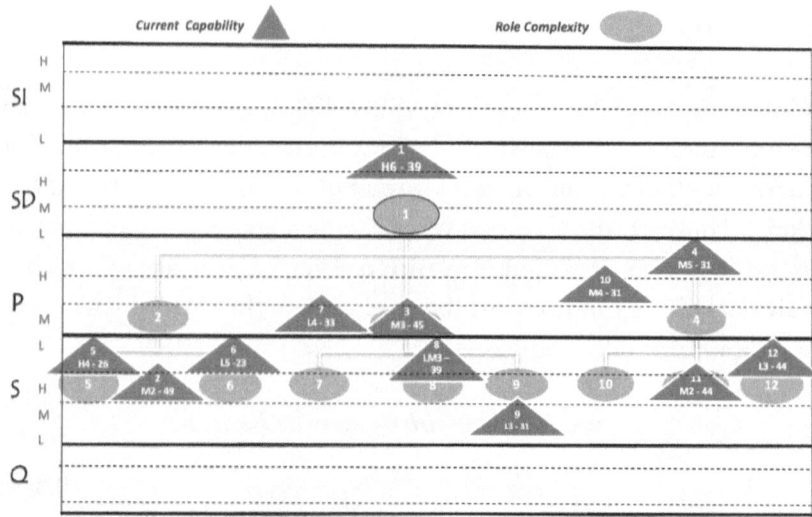

In the Organisational Map employees' capability results are reflected as **triangles**, and the complexity of their roles as **ovals**. One can thus determine from the map which employee's capability is congruent with the complexity of their roles, versus those which are not. For example, person 11 is likely to be experiencing flow, whilst person 1 is likely to feel somewhat underutilised.

Figure 3.10: Capability and Flow Balance Sheet

Level of Team	Team Size	ASSETS			LIABILITIES		
		Nr of Team in Flow	Flow		Nr of Team Out of Flow	Over-Stretched	Under-Utilized
3 (Practice)	10	4	40%		6	0%	60%
		Total Flow = 40%			Total Misuse = 60%		

In the Capability and Flow Balance sheet, it is evident that in this particular team 40% of the members are in flow and 60% are underutilised. Those in flow are considered **Assets** whereas those out of flow are **Liabilities**. The data for the Capability and Flow Balance Sheet is derived from the Organisational Map.

CREATING THE CONDITIONS FOR FLOW

Talent and Structural Analytics therefore provide organisations with an accurate view as to which employees are likely to be currently in flow from a capability perspective, and / or underutilised or overstretched.

Two questions, however, that need to be addressed by organisational talent specialists are:

1. How do we create the conditions for flow for those employees who are either underutilised or overstretched? (i.e., turning Liabilities into Assets)
2. How do we ensure that those employees currently in flow remain in flow over time? (i.e, ensuring Assets remain Assets).

Being able to answer these questions is critical for organisations to ensure that employees experience flow at work, feel fulfilled in their roles, and are thereby less likely to resign and / or quietly quit.

Employees who are Underutilised and / or Overstretched

There is obviously greater risk that these employees could resign or quietly quit given that they are out of flow. This is even more of a concern for the organisation when these employees have been assessed to have high future potential (as assessed by a capability assessment) and are considered part of the organisation's 'talent pool' for succession planning. It is reemphasised that capability assessments provide an overview of the future capability distribution in the organisation, and what their future talent pipeline looks like.

> ...capability assessments provide an overview of the future capability distribution in the organisation, and what their future talent pipeline looks like.

Employees who are **_underutilised_** in their current roles (i.e., their capability exceeds the complexity requirements of the role) are likely to feel bored and frustrated. They may feel they have more value to add to the organisation, however their role doesn't allow for this. Because they are unable to display their capability, they may resign and look to do so in another organisation, or, if they choose to stay, they may begin to interfere with others in the workplace and perhaps even encroach on their manager's work.

Alternatively, they quietly quit and do the bare minimum, resulting in their engagement, commitment, emotional state, productivity and performance all seeing a notable drop.

Obviously, any of these outcomes are undesirable for both the employee and the organisation.

Interventions Focussing on Underutilised Employees (Disuse)

Where employees are *underutilised*, the following interventions can be considered:

1. Career Conversations

Talent Specialists, HR Personnel or Line Managers should engage in career conversations with these employees. In these conversations, it is imperative to acknowledge the possibility that these individuals are out of flow and underutilised. This discourse should also focus on attaining a view of current performance, and their perspective on their current flow state.

Engaging with the employee in a forum such as this demonstrates appreciation of their unique situation and experience at work, and contributes to mitigating the negative effects of them being underutilised.

These conversations also provide an opportunity to discuss the ways in which the organisation can help create the conditions for the employees to find their flow, such as discussing their career ambitions in light of their potential, as well as transitions from one theme to the next. Additionally, other job opportunities within the structure, where there is alignment between the employee's capability and job complexity, as well as skills and experience can be unpacked.

Career conversations therefore provide a suitable platform from which to begin engaging with underutilised employees. This type of engagement is a necessary yet insufficient way of ensuring that the organisation retains these employees.

2. Coaching

Coaching is another intervention that can be used, which too provides a way of appreciating the challenges faced by underutilised employees. Coaching is very goal orientated in nature, and can therefore be very specific about what both the employee and organisation needs to do, in order to ensure the employees find flow at work once again. Career conversations are also very likely to be infused into the coaching process.

3. Adapting the Current Role or Creating something New

Another intervention that can be considered, though one which can be quite challenging in the context of the organisational structure, is to analyse the current role to determine if it can be adapted and made 'bigger' so that it becomes more 'complex' in nature. The challenge of doing this is that it impacts, not only the role, but the structure that the role is embedded in. Thus, this intervention can only be carried out successfully by applying a holistic and systemic view.

Alternatively, the organisation could consider creating a new role for the employee that is pitched at the right theme of complexity. This can also be challenging to achieve, and prior to implementation, the implications for strategy and structure needs to be considered.

4. Lateral Moves

In preparation for a vertical move (i.e, promotion) it may be useful to move employees laterally. Whilst this may not provide sufficient challenge from a complexity perspective, it will provide employees with an opportunity to learn new skills, accumulate more knowledge and experience, attain broader exposure, and provide some novelty and variety, which could reengage them for a period of time until they are ready for a vertical move.

5. Promotions

A very logical solution for the organisation is to determine whether or not there are any current or future promotional opportunities available. If there are no opportunities currently available, then consider lateral moves as per the above. Should promotion opportunities be currently available then experience, knowledge, and skills (in addition to capability) must be considered.

6. Exposure

Whilst in their current role, the organisation can provide employees with exposure to more complex work. This will at least provide the employees with more challenge and stimulation in the short term.

To increase exposure the following can be implemented:

- Increase learning opportunities through involving employees in projects at the next theme of work
- Provide the opportunity for job rotation and or / job shadowing
- Involve the employees in meetings, conferences and forums where content and discussions are pitched at the next theme of work
- Afford the employees the opportunity to work with a mentor who is already working at a more complex theme of work
- Send employees on relevant training that will stretch and stimulate them.

7. Management

The relationship between managers and employees is extremely important in the context of creating the conditions for flow. Managers who are able to establish an optimal working environment have both a greater chance of retaining underutilised employees and ensuring that these employees still perform despite being out of flow.

> The relationship between managers and employees is extremely important in the context of creating the conditions for flow.

BIOSS utilises the **Tripod of Work** management model to help foster strong relationships between managers and employees. **According to the Tripod of Work, managers need to be able to perform three activities effectively, namely Tasking, Trusting and Tending.** Managers who execute these activities effectively can create many positive outcomes, including establishing the optimal conditions for flow and engagement.

The Tripod of Work, and its relationship to flow will be discussed and unpacked in the next section.

8. Other Conditions for Flow

As mentioned previously, the concept of flow is multifaceted, and looking at the congruence between capability and complexity is just one component of the whole. For employees who are underutilised, management or talent specialists could additionally assess the other factors that impact flow. **As highlighted by Csíkszentmihályi (1990) the presence of clear goals, the availability of immediate feedback, ensuring the individual is sufficiently skilled, and has control and autonomy over their work situation, are other conditions that impact the flow state.**

In addition, further engagement factors can be considered, such as management / employee relationships, the working environment, ways of working (i.e., office-based, hybrid or remote working), and professional growth opportunities. Whilst these alone may be insufficient to retain and engage understimulated employees, they may at the very least ensure the organisation retains the service of the employees for longer, whilst implementing some of the above mentioned interventions to create flow.

9. Exiting

It is possible that the suggested interventions will not produce the desired result, and, in these situations, it may be better for the underutilised employee to resign and exit the business. If the boredom and frustration experienced is adversely affecting their decision making, productivity, and general performance, and all efforts to reengage them has been unsuccessful, it may be prudent for both the employee and organisation that the employee exits.

Interventions Focussing on Overstretched Employees (Misuse)

Employees who are ***overstretched*** in their current roles (i.e. the complexity requirements of the role exceed their capability) are likely to feel stressed, worried and perplexed. They are likely to have been promoted too early into a more complex role, and consequently will be overwhelmed with the decision-making requirements. Because they are unable to add value at the required theme of work, there is a good chance they will pull the level of work down to align with their capability, focus solely on responsibilities they are comfortable with, disengage altogether, or resign. All of these outcomes are undesirable.

For employees who are ***overstretched***, interventions similar to those outlined above can be considered, albeit their nature, content and process may differ.

1. Career Conversations

Career conversations with employees who are overstretched or overwhelmed are more sensitive in nature. These conversations will therefore need to be approached carefully and appreciatively with a focus on aspects such as job performance, career aspirations and ambitions. Conversations will need to be moulded around current capability and future potential, and what opportunities are available in the current structure where they could experience flow.

2. Coaching

If an employee has been overpromoted it is likely that he / she will be struggling to cope with the demands, responsibilities and outputs required of the role. In this context the coach, in the absence of other interventions, will focus on helping the employee to bridge whatever gaps can be bridged. This could involve strengthening current capability whilst providing exposure to more complex themes of work, as well as developing other skills and technical proficiencies for the role. The goal of the coaching will be to help the employee to cope with the demands of the role as much as possible, as well as to mitigate the organisational risks for as long as possible, whilst other related interventions are implemented.

3. Redeploying

Another intervention to consider is redeploying the employee into a different role in the structure that is aligned to the employee's capability. Whilst this can be a very effective intervention, it will depend on what the organisation requires in terms of the structure, and available vacancies.

4. Adapting the Current Role

This would involve an adaptation of the current role to align with the employee's capability. An analysis of the role outputs, responsibilities and accountabilities will need to take place, in order to determine the ways in which role could be transformed to reduce its complexity. As mentioned previously, adapting a job role to fit an employee's capability can be quite challenging in the context of the organisational structure.

5. Exiting

In the event that the discussed interventions are unsuccessful it may be prudent for both the employee and organisation that the employee resigns and exits the organisation. This course of action is particularly salient when the employee has been overpromoted into a strategic role where the consequences of poor decision-making and inadequate performance carries greater business risk.

Consideration for Employees in Flow

Employees in flow are considered to be organisational **Assets** and hence need to be nurtured to ensure they are retained and that the organisation gets the best out of them. In order to achieve this, organisations need to consider the following:

- Capability is fluid, and matures and grows naturally over time; therefore employees who are currently in flow may not be in the future. This implies that the **Assets** of today could become the **Liabilities** of tomorrow.
- Organisations therefore need to manage these individuals' careers closely by understanding how their capability will mature over time, and when employees are likely to transition from one theme of work to the next (i.e. talent readiness). In this way organisations will be better positioned to keep employees in flow as they mature along their growth curves.
- Whilst employees may be in flow with the complexity requirements of their roles, it does not necessarily mean they will be in flow with all components of their roles. Employees may find their experience of flow fluctuates depending on what tasks they are executing. It is almost impossible to be in flow all of the time and this reality needs to be communicated.
- It is important to acknowledge that employees' experience of flow and its associated positive outcomes could be adversely affected by other engagement factors (or the lack thereof), such as poor management and leadership, a toxic culture, a lack of feedback and recognition, limited growth and development opportunities, and an uninclusive work environment (Tenny, M; 2021). An example of this is an employee who is theoretically in flow, but disengages and performs poorly due to the toxic culture they work in.

THE BIOSS MANAGEMENT MODEL:
THE TRIPOD OF WORK

A key reason for the onset of the 'Great Resignation' and 'Quiet Quitting' is that employers, and in particular managers, have taken their employees for granted. This is evident in managers **not** providing enough of the following for their employees:

- Attention, support and care
- Work / job fulfilment
- Active listening
- Understanding as to how their work contributes to the organisation's overall purpose
- Autonomy and empowerment
- Sense of belonging and having a connection to others
- Healthy workplace culture

In relation to this, an article by Zenger and Folkman (2022) highlights the findings of data they have been collecting via 360 leadership assessments since 2020. They compared the results of more than 13 000 employees' ratings of 2801 managers. Their data revealed that 'managers who were rated highest on balancing relationships with results saw 62% of their employees willing to give extra effort and only 3% quietly quitting."

Zenger and Folkman therefore state the following: "Our data indicates that quiet quitting is usually less about an employee's willingness to work harder and more creatively, and more about a manager's ability to build a relationship with their employees where they are not counting the minutes until quitting time." In terms of managing quiet quitters, they highlight the importance of building trusting relationships between managers and employees and they point to the need to create safer, inclusive, more positive workplaces.

At the heart of the Tripod of Work model, is the acknowledgement and understanding that as organisations face significant and continuous change, the relationship between managers and employees, or leaders and team-members, comes into concentrated focus. This points to the importance of creating working environments where employees feel able to make a significant contribution to the success of their employing organisation. An important component of this is therefore centred around the nature of managerial / employee relationships. The Tripod of Work is a model and tool which helps to clarify these relationships.

Additionally, the model describes a way of establishing and sustaining the conditions for 'flow' for individuals in their context at work. Individuals with the responsibility for employees (i.e., leaders or managers) must be able to make provision for those who work for them to use their capabilities to the full.

The Tripod of Work model was developed by Gillian Stamp after many years of listening to vast numbers of employees talk and reflect on what they require from their managers to be successful, engaged and in flow at work (i.e., based on 150,000 conversations). It is therefore considered to be a useful and applicable model in the context of 'The Great Resignation' and 'Quiet Quitting' challenges that organisations are facing.

The model focuses on three key conditions that employees need and want to exist at work:

- To be clear about what is expected of them
- To feel that what they are doing is important and valuable
- To be allowed to decide for themselves how to get the work done

According to the Tripod of Work, managers therefore need to be able to perform the three Tripod of Work management activities effectively. These activities are:

1. **Tasking** – sharing dreams, aspirations, hopes, agreeing objectives in outputs by explaining what needs to be done, by when, to what standard. It is ultimately about ensuring that the strategic intent is clear for everyone involved in its implementation.
2. **Trusting** – Entrusting someone with the purposes of the organisation, and then trusting them to use their skill and

judgement to do the work. It's about ensuring people have the responsibility to use their judgement to achieve the expected outputs. To be fully motivated, individuals need to feel trusted to do their best, and that they are neither over-loaded in terms of what they can achieve, nor under-whelmed by the scope of the work they have been given.

3. **Tending** – Monitoring without interference: attending to what unfolds over time, checking resources, priorities and progress, and picking up early signs of opportunity and risk. Part of tending is to communicate a sense of purpose and relevance for the work so that all individuals have a context (a framework) within which to see their work. If the context changes, then employees need to have this information. This enables them to use their judgement to adjust in specific cases on their own initiative.

The essence of the Tripod is for leaders / managers to maintain the appropriate balance and tension between the three activities. In daily organisational life these three activities blend all the time, but for simplicity the model deals with them as three pairs:

- *Tasking and Trusting*

  When the balance between Tasking and Trusting appropriate, the organisation gets the best blend between deciding what things should be done and how best to do them. The output of this optimal balance is 'Organisational **Judgement**'.

- *Tasking and Tending*

  When this balance is appropriate, the organisation gets the best blend between keeping track of what is being done, how much it is costing, and, in the light of changes inside and outside the company, assessing whether it is still a good thing to be doing. This output is called 'Organisational **Review**'.

- ***Tending and Trusting***

  When this balance is appropriate, people are given time and attention, sufficient to keep them informed of the purpose and value of their work, so that - when suitable opportunities arise – they can use their judgement to improve the intended results. The output of this balance is called 'Organisational **Coherence**'.

When leaders / managers maintain the appropriate balance between the three activities, the **Optimal Tripod of Work** is produced.

The Optimal Tripod, as suggested by the name, is an optimal model of interaction between manager and team members that can create and maintain a working environment where people are freed to use their initiative through the bounding of judgement by tasking, encouraged through trusting, and feel supported by tending.

The Optimal Tripod can be seen in the figure below:

Figure 3.11: The Optimal Tripod

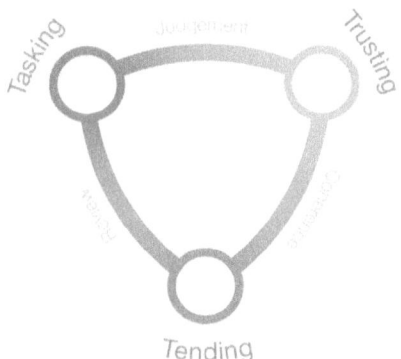

The Optimal Tripod is associated with the following positive outcomes:

- Effective employee judgement
- Creating coherence and effective review
- Creating the optimal conditions for flow and engagement
- Employee empowerment, autonomy, control, and self-confidence
- Increased employee willingness to go the extra mile
- Improved management culture and employee experience
- Enhanced employee performance and well-being
- Improved ability to manage in an agile work environment

It is therefore evident that creating Optimal Tripods will do much to help improve the relationships between leader / managers and their employees, thereby helping to mitigate the talent management and retention risks associated with the 'Great Resignation' and 'Quiet Quitting'.

Often, however, the particular environment of an organisation impacts its culture in a variety of ways that invariably influences the in-house style of management. This is particularly pronounced when organisations operate in turbulent, volatile, and unpredictable environments as has happened during the COVID-19 pandemic. Consequently, some organisational cultures may encourage sub-optimal and undesirable interactions - management styles that are either too rigid or too diffuse. Where we see a very rigid management style, the Rigid Tripod is produced and where the management style is too diffuse in nature, we see the Diffuse Tripod arising.

Within the Rigid Tripod, managers specify too much, control too tightly, and leave too little room for their people to use their discretion. Conversely, within the Diffuse Tripod, managers do not give sufficient clarity, enough framework or guidance to allow their people to understand what they need to do. Neither of these two Tripods is ideal, and it is very possible that the Covid pandemic and its aftermath have resulted in a number of Rigid and / or Diffuse Tripods developing, possibly even unintentionally in organisations, with the consequences contributing to resignations and quiet quitting.

The Rigid Tripod and Diffuse Tripods are shown below.

Figure 3.12: Rigid Tripod   *Figure 3.13: Diffuse Tripod*

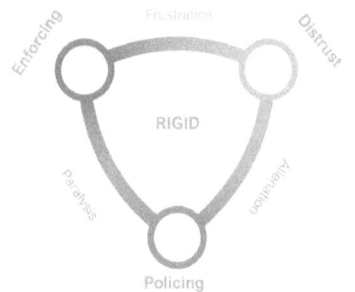
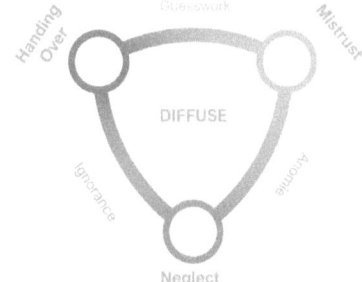

Useful tips, and considerations for Talent Management Professionals:

- Talent management and retention is made a lot easier when you have the right people in the right roles at the right time.
- Using capability assessments for selection purposes ensures you get this right at the outset when an employee joins the organisation.
- Implementing a Nature of Work Review (NoW) makes the process of matching employees to roles much easier, and in doing so, conditions for flow are created.
- In addition to helping establish the conditions for flow, NoW Reviews provide informative and diagnostic information on the state of a company's organisational structure (i.e., is it requisite or not? and if not, what needs to be adjusted?).
- Remember, employees want to be in flow! This makes their job roles more meaningful and allows them to perform optimally. In the flow state, work does not feel like work!
- Don't assume that all employees want to be operating at strategic levels. Employees want to be in flow and are often realistic and understand the type of work that will provide this for them.
- Levels of Work and job grading are different and are not always aligned.
- It is possible to be out of flow and still performing. In these cases, it is often due to the tenacity, grit and industriousness of

the employee. This may also be due to other engagement factors e.g., the employee fits the culture, has an attentive and supportive manager, is happy with working conditions, and feels aligned to the broader organisational purpose.

- Flow is multifaceted. Capability versus complexity is just one component of this.
- **Performance is not the same as Potential.** Just because an employee is performing doesn't mean she / he is ready to be promoted into a more complex role.
- Promote with current capability and future potential in mind, not just performance.
- When using assessments for selection and development purposes, multiple constructs should be assessed - not just capability in isolation. Other areas to assess include personality, emotional intelligence, cognition and integrity.
- If an employee is out of flow, there may be occasions when it is better for both the employee and the organisation that he / she resigns. Sometimes flow may only be found in a different role in a different organisation.

CONCLUSION

This chapter focused on two phenomena impacting organisations today due to COVID-19, namely 'The Great Resignation' and 'Quiet Quitting'.

Whilst there are different approaches that organisations can utilise to try to mitigate the adverse effects these two trends are having on talent management and retention, the author presented a unique methodology developed by BIOSS that can be adopted and implemented.

The author introduced readers to the BIOSS methodology, and the various models, theories and constructs that are part of its' DNA.

The chapter discussed BIOSS' approach to analysing both structure and people, leading to the generation of various talent and structural analyses, as a means to determine and create the conditions for employees to experience flow at work - thereby mitigating the adverse effects of the stated phenomena. Readers were introduced to the concept of Flow, the Matrix of Working Relationships (MWR), the constructs of capability and complexity, capability assessments, Nature of Work (NoW) Reviews, as well as interventions that can be utilised to establish the conditions for flow.

The second part of the chapter focused on BIOSS' management model called the Tripod of Work. This is a tool that can be utilised to enhance the relationships between managers and employees, or leaders and team-members and in doing so, establish the conditions for 'flow' for individuals at work.

Finally, the chapter presented some useful tips and considerations for talent management professionals in light of BIOSS' methodology, theories, and tools.

About Paul Leibowitz:

Paul holds an M. Com degree in Industrial / Organisational Psychology from the University of Cape Town, and is a registered Industrial / Organisational Psychologist with the Health Professional Council of South Africa (HPCSA). He has 17 years corporate consulting and assessment experience where he has consulted to some of the leading blue-chip organisations in South Africa. Additionally, Paul has worked with global companies in the Middle East, Russia, Brazil, Australia and further afield in Africa (i.e., Botswana, Namibia, and Kenya).

Paul is currently a director, partner, and shareholder in Bioss Southern Africa, which is a Business Psychology consulting business. Additionally, Paul is a director and shareholder of EDAC. EDAC is an assessment technology company based in Cyprus.

About Bioss SA:

BIOSS SA is a niche' consultancy focused on improving organisational and people effectiveness. This is achieved through a blend of assessment, consulting and technology solutions. Core lines of business are Psychometric, Capability and Gamified Assessments, Talent Management, Organisational Design, and Structural and Talent Analytics. The organisation has been successfully providing its products, services, and technology to clients since 1989 and the client base has steadily grown to over 200. Its offices are in Johannesburg and Cape Town and associate consultants in various local and global geographies.

CHAPTER FOUR

DISRUPTIVE MOMENT, DISRUPTIVE APPROACH

OVERVIEW

In managing talent-succession challenges, professionals are now faced with a curious dilemma regarding the expectations of business leaders and stakeholders. The disruptions created by the coronavirus pandemic have compelled talent custodians to adopt disruptive approaches to dealing with new world-of-work challenges.

Interestingly, out of these disruptions and challenges come varying opportunities. The question is, how do we position businesses to look beyond the challenges and begin to proactively leverage the opportunities that have been created?

With contextual reference to talent and talent management in organisations, I have defined a talent as, "an individual whose contributions directly help to achieve the core objectives of the organisation or business either now or in the future (or both)." I raised a question recently while discussing the way forward with regards to tackling some specific talent challenges which one of my clients operating in the professional service industry was facing. The question was, "Would the organisation rather focus on the capabilities or competencies required to deliver on current organisational goals or should the focus be on the future strategic ambitions of the organisation?" This question was relevant because the focus would largely impact the pool of talents which the organisation would desire to attract and retain. The majority of executives at this session favoured a split between a focus on what I tagged "the now" and "the future." However, two of the executives (out of seven that were present) tilted their arguments towards a focus on "the now." They justified this with an explanation that as a professional service firm, it would make more business sense to strictly focus on tackling the current situations facing the firm including, matching the clients' expectations with satisfactory services such that they would not have any reason to look for alternatives. Additionally, this focus would allow them to attract more clients, particularly through referrals, thereby managing the future on a day-by-day basis. This posture could be considered a deliberate choice or strategy. After all, a strategy is a "choice." Disruptive talent management approaches require a deliberate choice amongst varying options with due consideration for the overall alignment with the strategic intent of the organisation.

Conventionally, we are used to the sequential approach to talent management. This means, we have often followed a structured step-by-step process in dealing with the talent-succession needs of a business; we look at the business' goals, identify critical roles in the organisation, review the incumbents in such roles, identify and review successors to the roles (including, their potential, performance, knowledge, skills and others) then, figure out the development interventions (based on identified gaps) that will enable the identified individuals (talents) to transition into the critical roles seamlessly. We try to proactively manage the future vacancy/succession risks. As great as the sequential approach to talent management is (note that this is absolutely still relevant in the talent-succession process), COVID-19 has taught us a few lessons:

- If you fail to plan in disruptive times, your organisation or business could be stranded.
- Disruptive moments call for disruptive talent management actions.

Disruptive times bring about uncommon leaders and unexpected leadership transitions. During disruptive times, even the leaders you thought were prepared to take on leadership roles could be hindered from assuming these roles. We witnessed this during the COVID-19 lockdowns. Mobility restrictions and other contending or limiting circumstances could occur even when an organisation has all the resources to mobilise. The talent or individual who has been prepared to assume a key role may no longer be willing to be mobilised due to personal constraints including the "fear factor," happenings within the environment or a total change in the career preference of the individual. A decision to opt for a career preference with a different pattern which allows the individual to align work with a balanced life could have also triggered the opting out of the talent from succession or leadership role.

EMERGENCE OF UNCOMMON LEADERS

Disruptions, including those witnessed during COVID-19 have triggered the emergence of leaders who ordinarily, would not have come on the scene if things were normal. Though I mentioned in the previous chapters how the events of COVID-19 triggered various sensemaking and uncommon actions by both employees and employers, it is important to further explore the situation from the organisational standpoint. In building the resilience required to navigate the prevailing circumstances and remain in business, many organisations focused on various adaptive strategies.

From the employer's standpoint, putting strategies in place to harness the existing core skills within the business has now become a priority and a challenge at the same time. While high-potential talents are given opportunities for stretched assignments, individuals with reduced value additions to the business' goals and are considered to have reached their peak (vis-à-vis their skills sets) are strategically managed out of the organisation. This pattern has encouraged "uncommon role holders" with a multiplicity of core and transferable skills to emerge. These uncommon role holders are now given rare opportunities to assume positions which they previously would not have been considered for but for the disruptions their employers are trying to mitigate to remain in business.

SCENARIO: DIALOGUE WITH AN EXECUTIVE

I had a conversation with a senior executive of a leading global company in the energy and gas value chain. This organisation was of particular interest to me because I was privy to their deliberate and robust talent-succession approach which has enabled the organisation to develop and transition leaders – particularly locals – into roles which could have been occupied by expatriates. Although this organisation has a sizable number of expatriates in various roles, their deliberateness in succession planning is admirable. This organisation adopts a "disclosure approach" to managing identified successors to critical roles. The executive who engaged in the dialogue with me was notified of his next level transition about a year before he assumed the role. However, years before the transition was implemented, this executive had been assigned various high visibility and challenging assignments. A year before his new role as managing director, he was invited to an executive chat which ended with him being handed a one-year development plan to facilitate his transition into the managing director role. In view of the transitional plan, this executive was also tasked with preparing a successor for his current role to ensure that his transition would not create an undesired vacancy or leadership risk.

It became of interest to me to have a conversation with the executive (who had already assumed the managing director role at this stage) to understand some of the adaptive strategies that his company adopted to remain relevant in the midst of the disruptions caused by COVID-19. Our dialogue commenced with me setting the context to ensure we achieved the expected goals. Excerpts of our conversation are reflected in the rest of this chapter.

Dialogue Context

When certain organisations consider the talent management process as a critical business process, we do not take it for granted. Apparently not every organisation understands the implications of how neglecting this process affects their overall business continuity. Many organisations tend to be reactive in their approach. No doubt, failing to adopt or implement a talent management strategy has wide-ranging impacts on an organisation regardless of its size or the sector in which it operates. Therefore, with the experiences and facts that have emerged from the COVID-19 pandemic, I asked my client the following questions:

i.   How did your organisation keep business running amid restrictions and global lockdowns, since your organisation is largely involved in cross-talent mobility across countries?

ii. In your view, how did COVID-19 redefine your talent management approach. How did the events of COVID-19 trigger a new wave of future leaders in your organisation?

iii. Is the workforce of yesterday still the same as that of the future?

iv. What role has technology played in your organisation so far and how would it impact the future?

v.   And finally, what kind of support was available to employees to cope with instances such as mental illnesses, loneliness, and the feelings of isolation, which some employees experienced during the pandemic?

During the conversation, we agreed that the experiences of COVID-19 influenced several employees to rediscover themselves. In turn, these rediscoveries posed immense challenges on various organisations to redesign their talent-succession approach by introducing various coping strategies

> **Managing career transitions in the midst of chaos is a challenge.**

including enhanced work flexibility. Managing career transitions in the midst of chaos became a challenge. Organisations realised that the pandemic experience has also shifted or shaped the way employees perceive careers. An instance was referenced where an organisation asked their employees to return to the office after the relaxation of COVID-19 restrictions and several employees resisted this plan. They raised concerns about returning to a five-day, eight-to-five, work week. They asked the organisation to consider a staggered work plan or flexible working arrangements as many of them would be willing to quit if the organisation insisted on continuing pre-pandemic work schedules.

Several employees enjoyed the benefits of extended family bonding thanks to option to "work-from-home" during the COVID-19 lockdowns. Employees have generally developed a keen appreciation of the benefits of having a balanced work life. This experience has made the workforce interpret the concept of work differently. Before now, the workplace was largely restricted to the four walls of offices. But new patterns have emerged including the concept of home offices. So, how do we now define work given its evolution in various dimensions? People work remotely and attend important meetings from their cars; in several instances, many chauffeurs have become part of an executive's work team. So, **both employers and employees have been faced with a lot of post-pandemic dilemmas despite the opportunities that have also been created.**

Furthermore, as the discussion progressed, the executive's views were aligned with the fact that many businesses have been forced to deploy ingenious interventions to stay in business. Managing the organisation's key talents and ensuring the relevance of every member of the workforce in alignment with the organisation's strategic intents have become a priority. Consequently, many businesses have redefined how they work and the workspaces they occupy (mostly driven by the opportunity to save costs and support employees' emerging preferences).

Impact on the Business and Call for Action

As stated by the executive, in the world of work and as a business leader, it is important to find ways to control costs while driving employee engagement. This was one area he grappled with during the pandemic. The entire business world was resorting to job cuts in some sectors to cope with the challenges at the time, and he was faced with a dilemma of controlling cost while attending to the needs of his employees.

The executive considers himself an executional strategist therefore, the success of his business required an immediate and practical approach. To drive his executional strategy at the height of the pandemic, he decided it was more important to focus on getting the job done and not who was doing the job. He understood that to grow as a leader, you must pass on the knowledge, empower your people and back them up. Collaboration, team-working and team trust are crucial to driving the executional strategy, particularly, in a disruptive circumstance. In his opinion, COVID-19 caught every business leader unawares, nobody knew exactly what to do.

The executive also addressed questions around, how the pandemic impacted him personally as well as the business he leads". He had employees who needed to be out on the field in different parts of the country, in remote areas, in offshore locations, in land assets, in not easily accessible areas as they all push to deliver value to clients. As a business, his company provides power infrastructure, their customers are multinational oil and gas companies, large industrial corporations, and manufacturers who are required to keep their operations running to support not just their clients but the country at large. Also, due to their services and business support to independent power plants, it was difficult to halt their operations during the pandemic. Therefore, they had the burning challenge of figuring out how to immediately set up a network of employees who could be deployed across the country to customers' locations while protecting them from getting infected with COVID-19. At the time, there was no vaccine, testing facility and or cure for COVID-19, so a lot was riding on trial and error. However, the executive had to maintain a disposition of steadiness and calm even though, he was certain it was not going to be easy.

> **Collaboration, team-working and team trust are crucial to driving the executional strategy, particularly, in a disruptive circumstance.**

There were a couple of motivations at play here. There was the obvious need to generate revenue for the company while managing these unforeseen circumstances. But more importantly, was the need to keep employees safe and ensure they would return to their families safe and healthy without the fear of potentially infecting their families with the virus. So, the focus was underpinned by two main perspectives – creating value for the employee and for the organisation.

Furthermore, this business operates in a sector where knowledge and expertise are very diverse. About 30 percent of their workforce were highly technical experts who had to be recruited from overseas to work with the 70 percent local workforce, who were also technical/field staff. As a global organisation, a lot of their experts are spread across various countries in different parts of the world. In most cases, this expert pool is deployed as a shared service. This means, instead of replicating their highly specialised roles in every region in which they operate, the company would contact their resource pool within the shared services and assign individuals to support its operations as may be required. However, due to mobility restrictions/lockdowns imposed by COVID-19, this team of shared services resources was unavailable to physically support global business operations. The executive determined that the most appropriate solution was to maximize the potential inherent in the 70 percent of his local workforce to deliver maximum value for their clients/customers.

His first step was to heavily leverage technology to conduct remote training to bridge the skills gap/s for all the employees. The trainings were segmented in line with the various functions each employee was tasked to perform. Especially for the logistics personnel and technical (field) staff who were going to be deployed physically or had already been deployed to offshore or remote locations to support the company's huge client base. Note that at the time, air travels were totally restricted, and the business was limited to approving essential travel which was only possible by road. This became very chaotic for business operations. Despite being able to secure the required government permits to move essential employees and required equipment by road, while abiding by COVID-19 protocols, it was a herculean task for the business to manage these unusual disruptions as most of its existing operations structures were distabilised.

The executive stayed focused on his strategy to get the job done and not be too concerned about who was doing the work. As a matter of urgency, he identified key individuals amongst the 70 percent of the workforce that could take on additional responsibilities. Leveraging technology, he created virtual technical buddies comprising overseas experts and local employees. With this technical buddy process, the overseas experts were able to provide guided, high-level support to local technical employees. This allowed them to use various complex, technical instruments through virtual guidance and remote diagnostics support. Field technical workers were able to follow the instructions and guidance being provided virtually to carry out various complex tasks. They would not have had this opportunity without the disruptions caused by COVID-19. Many of the employees were able to learn quickly, improve their on-the-job experience and increase their confidence levels. This technology transfer in an extremely challenging situation produced impressive, positive results. Eventually, "uncommon leaders" and "high-potential individuals" emerged within the organisation through this process. Subsequently, upon review of this process, it helped the organisation develop a support solution which has now become its operations template. This is now being implemented across their global business operations to deliver great value to their customers.

Calmness in the face of adversity

Individuals will face various adversities while building viable careers. However, from the conversation with this executive, it is clear that while tackling any challenge as a professional, staying calm in the face of challenges is key. In addition, being proactive in managing the challenge is also very important and this is in sync with the preemptive or anticipative skills required of any business leader.

Three main themes emerged from the experience shared by the executive. First, the need to generate revenue for the business despite major disruptions. Secondly, the desire to create value for employees in the face of the pandemic. Thirdly, the commitment towards ensuring the safety of employees while trying to manage business challenges. In aligning these themes, employees are positioned to take on both immediate and future business challenges, the organisation is poised to thrive and fulfil its business obligations and finally, the safety concerns within the business taken care of in the process.

This experience reemphasizes the importance of adopting a holistic approach to talent development. Particularly:

a) Integrating on-the-job training with employee development.
b) Leveraging technology to improve organisational learning and growth.
c) Developing local talent pools including successors prepared for critical roles.
d) Driving employee engagement by providing meaningful jobs and stretched assignments.
e) Ensuring the talent pipeline or benchstrength is viable such that the organisation can mitigate or manage any impending talent or vacancy risks. This also impacts the kind of individuals that the organisation hires or considers for the "feeder roles."

Furthermore, my conversation with the executive highlighted the fact that organisations will often find a way to navigate challenges and sustain the business into the future. And this aspiration typically leads to taking "not-so-common" decisions. As revealed by the executive, following the events of COVID-19, the business decided to merge certain functions/roles and provided opportunities for high-potential individuals – who had both the desire and ability – to assume complex roles. Eventually, those employees who did not fit the skills requirements at this stage were managed out of the organisation. The executive stated that based on the lessons from COVID-19, it became apparent that the business world would begin to clamour for a workforce of highfliers with complementary and transferable skills. These career-minded individuals would possess the resilience to deliver business goals under challenging situations. They will be tough and flexible individuals, capable of divergent thinking and with a can-do attitude. These employees will be able to adapt quickly in the face of contending business challenges.

To thrive into the future, business leaders need to identify talents who are resilient, individuals who can "work in a structured environment but have an unstructured mindset." Individuals with an unstructured mindset, who are open to challenges and will not rigidly follow the status quo i.e., "this is how we have always done it and must continue to do it." They are open-minded talents. **The new world of work also requires technology-savvy and technology-driven individuals, people who break barriers, communicate effectively in the face of challenges, and have a high level of interpersonal and relationship skills.**

For this executive, COVID-19 has redefined the talent management strategy of his company. They had to respond to business challenges using unconventional methods of identifying and developing talents. To put it simply, **the coronavirus pandemic triggered an unstructured approach to talent management.** The company's ingenious interventions as well as the support structures it provided, created a new breed of next level managers who were empowered to deliver the expected business results.

WRAP-UP

In conclusion, the executive stated that following from these experiences, his company has developed a sense of urgency for creating a succession pool for all the key roles that support the business. Business leaders have been charged with ensuring that they give focused attention to building viable successors across a wide range of business functions. And this succession planning mandate has been cascaded to form part of the scorecard for each business leader. Leaders across the organisation understand that no business can survive during a pandemic without a focused and deliberate talent management approach. Therefore, developing the next level of business leaders is now a performance measure across the organisation.

Additionally, workplace structures have been redefined compared to the pre-COVID era. Flexible work patterns have been embraced, the workforce is being empowered to troubleshoot basic IT challenges and proffer solutions while working remotely.

It should be mentioned that in today's workplace, team trust is critical for performance. As employees work remotely, team members and managers alike need to jettison micromanagement and trust that individual team members will deliver expected results once goals or deliverables are properly defined, communicated, and measured.

For aspiring leaders, do note that the future may not be known as we experienced with COVID-19. Therefore, be ready for the unexpected. Resilience, flexibility, and the ability to navigate uncertainties will be key leadership ingredients. You may take decisions that could end up being a mistake, however, being able to recognise an error of judgement and rebound quickly and strongly with renewed viguor will be required. Build your team through effective communication, share your vision, empower your team, and trust them to deliver on expected goals. Where performance gaps are identified, deploy the right intervention/s to close the gap/s.

CHAPTER FIVE

CONNECTING THE DOTS

OVERVIEW

The world of work has become unconventional hence, the work, workforce and workplace have aligned accordingly. I mentioned in the first edition of this book that, "an absence of effective talent management processes could amount to a journey towards a recession". I positioned that a recession is not only tied to a decline in economic activity or prosperity, but also related to a decline in the ability of any organisation to attract and deploy the needed talent due to prevailing constraints. Therefore, it is the strategic responsibility of any organisation to institutionalise a holistic talent-succession strategy that empowers the organisation to effectively manage its talent demand and supply. <u>If you want to see your businesses thrive into the future, you cannot afford to postpone or keep postponing your plan and effort towards institutionalising a viable talent management process.</u>

Talent management has become a critical business process. Therefore, organisations need to identify the appropriate strategy that delivers on their overall talent agenda. Whether the organisation decides to adopt the "buy", "build", "borrow" or any other adaptable approach, the overall talent goal for the business should be the focus. Also, the customisation of employee experience has become a major approach to talent management and must be embraced by employers. The professional wellbeing, financial wellbeing and work-life wellbeing of employees have all become a combined value proposition in the world of work. High value talents want to earn decent wages to sustain their needs, build progressive careers, and spend valuable time on other areas of interest, to promote total wellbeing development.

While the events of COVID-19 continue to unfold, various work patterns also keep emerging including situations where employees now seem to be influencing their employment contracts to fit with their career stages and preferences. In many ways, the power dynamic appears to be shifting in favour of employees. Especially, with the opportunities provided by technological inventions and advancements. The knowledge-worker and tech-driven workforce seems to be dictating the pace. Remote working has made the entire globe a single job market, individuals with complementary skills now juggle various jobs with multiple contracts. This trend has also enabled employers to manage the costs of workspaces, office overheads and other associated employee costs which would have been incurred if conventional (pre-pandemic) work patterns continued to be predominant.

The majority of the workforce pool seems to have personalised their careers and what career progression looks like for them. At the early stages of an individual's career, the pace of progression may appear to be constant. Individuals are likely to be flexible with career mobility and handling additional workloads. However, as the years roll by, employee preferences begin to shift, as they contend with other factors they consider to be important in their lives. Hence, the tendency to slow down and opt for a career that aligns with considerations for professional, financial, and work-life wellbeing.

MOVING FORWARD...

Generally, careers are characterised by interruptions, but what the world of work witnessed in the wake of the COVID-19 disruptions was unprecedented. The sense making outcomes of the pandemic have influenced career individuals to reposition themselves in order to proactively mitigate any future career chaos or shocks. We could say that, the events have triggered an improved ability to adapt to the environment by being emotionally aware and in control.

It is therefore imperative to:

i. Devise a means to "ring-fence" the "uncommon leaders" that have emerged within the organisational system as a result of the pandemic experience. Organisations have to continue to provide challenging jobs and a system which continuously ignites aspirational drive amongst top talents.

ii. Adopt relevant talent assessment and development interventions that provide valuable talent data for the purpose of understanding and taking the right steps in managing various transitional phases of high-potential individuals.

iii. Localise critical roles as much as practicable. During the global lockdown event, several organisations had no other choice than to allow the local workforce to occupy roles which would ordinarily have been manned by expatriates if not for the lockdowns. Many organisations were forced to bet on their local talent and several of them recorded immense successes. Now is the time to institutionalise this process, identify and breed local pools of successors as this will protect the organisation from any unplanned vacancy risk and leadership gap.

iv. Position businesses and their talent management approaches to look beyond the challenges and begin to proactively leverage the opportunities that have been created.

v. Utilise an integrated approach to mitigate the adverse effects that the "Great Resignation" and "Quiet Quitting" trends are having on talent management and retention.

vi. Effectively evaluate the work complexity as well as an assessment of individual capabilities to determine whether an employee is likely to be "in flow".

Work must be meaningful and challenging. The workforce mix must be such that it helps individuals to grow and be nurtured to achieve their career desires, provided it aligns with the overall organisational goals. Finally, the workplace is now as redefined as we are currently witnessing. Organisations need to be adaptable and provide the right organisational structures to support the workforce in delivering the expected results in the newly defined workplace.

ACKNOWLEDGEMENTS

We now have a fuller appreciation of the age long saying, "change is the only constant in life." I want to acknowledge the fact that COVID-19 impelled interesting change and dimensions to how we view the strategic importance of the talent management process. For me, the events of COVID-19 have reinvigorated my passion to continue to drive and support organisations in getting it right with their talent-succession agenda. I am very grateful to everyone who shared their personal experiences and talent-succession stories with me pre, during and post the COVID-19 pandemic. I achieved the second edition of this book through the insights they provided.

To my professional colleagues and friends, Christo van Staden, Seun Suleiman, Khairy Abuljebain, Lester Coupland, Paul Leibowitz and Joseph Atatsi, thank you for always encouraging me to push myself beyond my perceived boundaries. I am also, grateful for various opportunities provided by Kamal Abdalla Hidaytalla, Badredin Abdulmajeed, Eniola Ladapo, Olusegun Dada, Benedicta Ezeh, and Eniola Arausi. These opportunities have increased my learning and enriched my knowledge across sectors and cultures.

Even amid the pandemic, the Group Managing Director of Century Group, Ken Etete gave me a rare opportunity to contribute my quota by leading the group's human capital development. For the constant coaching and support by Executive Director of Century Group, Alaba Owoyemi to keep the fire burning, I am grateful. Faith Ideh, you have always been reliable in supporting the editing of my publications, well done.

My family has always been there all the way; Glory, Gift and Fortune, thank you for your endurance and encouragement on this career journey.

BIBLIOGRAPHY

Sources Cited in This Book:

Akinloye, A., (2020). Talent management agenda in a post Covid-19 world: A practical talent and succession management guide for professionals, executives, and business leaders. IN: AuthorHouse

Akinloye, A., (2010). Is Time Taken Off Work By Women During Maternity Leave A Career Hindrance? (A case study of some Nigerian Career women). Masters thesis submitted in partial fulfilment of the requirements for the degree of Master of Science, International HRM, Cranfield University, UK.

Akkermans, J., Seibert, S. E., and Mol, S. T., (2018). Tales of the Unexpected: Integrating Career Shocks in the Contemporary Careers Literature. SA Journal of Industrial Psychology 44: a1503. doi:10.4102/sajip.v44i0.1503.

Akkermans, J., Richardson, J., & Kraimer, M. (2020). The Covid-19 crisis as a career shock: Implications for careers and vocational behavior. Journal of Vocational Behaviour, 119,103434. https://doi.org/10.1016/j.jvb.2020.103434

Arthur, M., Hall, D., and Lawrence, B. (1989). Generating new directions in career theory: the case for transdisciplinary approach.

Benko, C. and Weisberg, A. (2007), "Implementing a corporate career lattice: the Mass Career Customization model", Strategy & Leadership, vol. 35, no. 5, pp. 29.

Birt, J. (2022, February 14). 14 Qualities of a Fulfilling Job (With Tips To Find One. Indeed. https://www.indeed.com/career-advice/finding-a-job/find-fulfilling-job

Blustein, D. L. (2019). The importance of work in an age of uncertainty: The eroding work experience in America. NY: Oxford University Press.

Blustein, D. L., Duffy, R., Ferreira, J. A., Cohen-Scali, V., Cinamon, R. G., and Allan, B. A., (2020). Unemployment in the time of COVID-19: A research agenda: Journal of Vocational Behavior 119 (2020) 103436.

Breitling, F., Dhar, J, Ebeling, R, & Lovich, D. (2021, November 15). 6 Strategies to Boost Retention Through the Great Resignation. *Harvard Business Review.* https://hbr.org/2021/11/6-strategies-to-boost-retention-through-the-great-resignation

Carden, L. (2007), Pathways to success for moderately defined careers: A study of relationships among prestige/autonomy, job satisfaction, career commitment, career path, training and learning, and performance as perceived by project managers (unpublished Ph.D. thesis), Texas A&M University, United States -- Texas.

Cesinger, K. (2022, September 4). What is quiet quitting? TikTok trend gets people talking about work ethic, setting boundaries. *ABC Eyewitness News.* https://abc7chicago.com/what-is-quiet-quitting-tiktok-video-covid-illinois-social-media/12194743/

Cho, E. (2020). Examining boundaries to understand the impact of COVID-19 on vocational behaviors: Journal of Vocational Behavior 119 (2020) 103437

Cholteeva, Y. (2022, August 8). 'Quiet quitting': how should HR manage it? *People Management.* https://www.peoplemanagement.co.uk/

article/1795213/quiet-quitting-hr-manageit?bulletin=pmdaily&utm_source=mc&utm_medium=email&utm_content=PM_Daily_08082022. https://www.peoplemanagement.co.uk/article/1795213/quiet-quitting-hr-manage-it%3Fbulletin%3Dpm-daily&utm_campaign=7295441&utm_term=5833448

Cooke, F.L., Dickmann, M., & Parry, E. (2021) IJHRM after 30 years: taking stock in times of COVID-19 and looking towards the future of HR research, The International Journal of Human Resource Management, 32:1, 1-23, DOI:10.1080/09585192.2020.1833070.

Cox, J. (2020a). Jobless claims soar past 3 million to record high. CNBC. Retrieved from https://www.cnbc.com/2020/03/26/weekly-jobless-claims.html.

Cox, J. (2020b). Coronavirus job losses could total 47 million, unemployment rate may hit 32%, fed estimates. CNBC. Retrieved from: https://www.cnbc.com/2020/03/30/coronavirus-job-losses-could-total-47-million-unemployment-rate-of- 32percent-fed-says.html.

De Gulan, X. M., & Aguiling, H. M. (2021). Developing a strategic career development model on organizational climate, career adaptability and career intentions.

Dickmann, M., & Bader, B. (2020). Global Mobility's response to COVID-19: Special issue RES Forum Research, June 2020

EFL Associates Executive Search & Talent Acquisition Blog. (2021, October 29). 6 Strategies to Combat the Great Resignation. https://eflassociates.cbiz.com/blog/artmid/28553/articleid/180/6-strategies-to-combat-the-great-resignation

El-Sabaa, S. (2001). The skills and career path of an effective project manager. International Journal of Project Management, 19, 1-7.

Ferreira, J. A., Reitzle, M., Lee, B., Freitas, R. A., Santos, E. R., Alcoforado, L., & Vondracek, F. W. (2015). Configurations of unemployment, reemployment, and psychological well-being: A longitudinal study of unemployed individuals in Portugal. Journal of Vocational Behavior, 91, 54–64. https://doi.org/10.1016/j.jvb.2015.09.004.

Foster, A. (2022, August 2). The surprising origin of the 'quiet quitting' trend sweeping multiple countries. *New York Post.* https://nypost.com/2022/08/02/the-surprising-origin-of-the-quiet-quitting-trend-sweeping-multiple-countries/

Fouad, N. A., & Bynner, J. (2008). Work transitions. American Psychologist, 63(4), 241–251.

Fouad, N. A., (2020). Editor in Chief's Introduction to Essays on the Impact of COVID-19 on Work and Workers. Journal of Vocational Behavior 119 (2020) 103441

Fox, M. (2022, May 10). The Great Resignation has changed the workplace for good. 'We're not going back,' says the expert who coined the term. *FOXCNBC.* https://www.cnbc.com/2022/05/10/-the-great-resignation-has-changed-the-workplace-for-good-.html

Friedman, Z. (2020). "How COVID-19 Will Change the Future of Work." Forbes, May 6. https://www.forbes.com/sites/zackfriedman/2020/05/06/covid-19-future-of-work-coronavirus/#5b1320a273b2

Giobbe, D. (1996) Conflict that tears at many women, New York: Jan 13, 1996. Vol 129, Iss 2; pg. 10

Golden, T. D., & Eddleston, K. A. (2020). Is there a price telecommuters pay? Examining the relationship between telecommuting and objective career success. Journal of Vocational Behavior, 116, 103348. https://doi.org/10.1016/j.jvb.2019.103348.

Grant, A. (2022) (Twitter). 26 August. Available at: https://twitter.com/AdamMGrant/status/1563164741987893248?ref_src=twsrc%5Etfw%7Ctwcamp%5Etweetembed%7Ctwterm%5E1563164741987893248%7Ctwgr%5Ef65555d55401637214dbb3bfccdae83dac7

6669e%7Ctwcon%5Es1_&ref_url=https%3A%2F%2Finmashable. com%2Ftech%2F37618%2Fwhat-is-quiet-quitting-why-are-major-companies-worried-about-this-bizarre-phenomenon. Accessed 28 September 2022).

Guan, Y., Deng, H., & Zhou, X. (2020). Understanding the impact of the COVID-19 pandemic on career development: Insights from cultural psychology. Journal of Vocational Behavior, 119, pg.1

Hedge, J., & Reneer, J. (2017). Improving Career Development Opportunities Through Rigorous Career Pathways Research. RTI Press Publication No. OP-0037-1703. Research Triangle Park, NC: RTI Press. doi.org/10.3768/rtipress.2017.op.0037.1703

Hite, L. M. & McDonald, K. S. (2020). Careers after COVID-19: challenges and changes, Human Resource Development International, 23:4, 427-437, DOI:10.1080/13678868.2020.1779576

Huffington, A. (2022, August). (Post). LinkedIn. https://www. linkedin.com/feed/update/urn:li:activity:6965397668625805312/ ?updateEntityUrn=urn:li:fs_feedUpdate:(V2,urn:li:activity:69653976 68625805312)&src=aff-ref&trk=aff-ir_progid%3D8005_ partid%3D10078_sid%3D_adid%3D449670&clickid=xhoSUrSi FxyIWgcQIFylmX2%3AUkDRW91oKSCSy00&mcid= 6851962469594763264&irgwc=1

International Labor Organization (2020a). ILO monitor: COVID-19 and the world of work. Third edition updated estimates and analysis. Retrieved May 5, 2020 from: https://www.ilo.org/wcmsp5/groups/ public/@dgreports/@dcomm/documents/briefingnote/wcms_743146.pdf.

International Labor Organization. (2020b). Young workers will be hit hard by COVID-19's economic fallout. https://iloblog.org/2020/04/15/ young-workers-will-behit-hard-by-covid-19s-economic-fallout/.

Johns Hopkins University (2022). Update Retrieved June 11, 2022 from: https://coronavirus.jhu.edu/map.html

Kalleberg, A. L. (2000). Nonstandard employment relations: Part-time, temporary and contract work. Annual Review of Sociology, 26, 341–365.

Kaplan, S., Engelsted, L., Lei, X., & Lockwood, K. (2018). Unpackaging manager mistrust in allowing telework: Comparing and integrating theoretical perspectives. Journal of Business and Psychology, 33(3), 365–382. https://doi.org/10.1007/s10869-017-9498-5.

Kramer, M. W. (1999). Motivation to reduce uncertainty: A reconceptualization of uncertainty reduction theory. Management Communication Quarterly, 13(2), 305–316. https://doi.org/10.1177/0893318999132007.

Kramer, A., & Kramer, K. Z. (2020). The potential impact of the Covid-19 pandemic on occupational status, work from home, and occupational mobility: Journal of Vocational Behavior 119 (2020) 103442

Kudhail, P. (2022, August 31). Quiet quitting: The workplace trend taking over TikTok. *BBC News*. https://www.bbc.com/news/business-62638908

Kvale, S. and Brinkmann, S. 2008. Interviewers: Learning the Craft of Qualitative Research Interviewing. Sage Publication Inc. London.

Lazarus, R. S., & Folkman, S. (1984). Stress, appraisal, and coping. New York: Springer.

Lindor, C. (2019, August 23). Council post: Five ways to invest in outgoing employees and benefit your organization. Forbes. https://www.forbes.com/sites/forbescoachescouncil/2019/08/23/five-ways-to-invest-in-outgoing-employees-and-benefit-your-organization/

Lund, S., Ellingrud, K., Hancock, B., and Manyika, J. (2020), April. "COVID-19 and Jobs: Monitoring the US Impact on People and Places." McKinsey Global Institute website. https://www.mckinsey.com/industries/public-sector/our-insights/covid-19-and-jobs-monitoring-the-us-impacton-people-and-places

Mainiero, L.A. and Sullivan, S.E. (2005), "Kaleidoscope careers: an alternative explanation for the 'Opt-out' Revolution". Academy of Management Executive, Vol 19, No 1, pg. 106-23

Nigeria Centre for Disease Control (2022). Update Retreived June 11, 2022 from: https://covid19.ncdc.gov.ng/#!

Noakes, J., & Landmann, J. (2021, December 13). The 'Great Resignation': A Global Risk? *Norton Rose Fulbright.* https://www.nortonrosefulbright.com/en-za/knowledge/publications/cc03a277/the-great-resignation-a-global-risk

Paul, K. I., & Moser, K. (2009). Unemployment impairs mental health: Meta-analyses. Journal of Vocational Behavior, 74, 264–282.

Pinker, J. (2020). The pandemic will cleave America in two. The Atlantic.

PwC's Global Workforce Hopes and Fears Survey. (2022, May, 24). https://www.pwc.com/gx/en/issues/workforce/hopes-and-fears-2022.html

Powell, O., (2021, February 11). How to mitigate the effects of The Great Resignation. *CX Network.* https://www.cxnetwork.com/cx-employee-engagement/articles/how-to-mitigate-the-effects-of-the-great-resignation

Rothbaum, F., Weisz, J. R., & Snyder, S. S. (1982). Changing the world and changing the self: A two-process model of perceived control. Journal of Personality and Social Psychology, 42(1), 5–37.

Salcedo, A., Yar, S., & Cherelus, G. (2020). Coronavirus travel restrictions, across the globe. New York Times. Retrieved from https://www.nytimes.com/article/coronavirus-travel-restrictions.html.

Seibert, S. E., Kraimer, M. L., & Heslin, P. A. (2016). Developing career resilience and adaptability. Organizational Dynamics, 45(3), 245–257. https://doi.org/10.1016/j.orgdyn.2016.07.009

Seibert, S. E., Kraimer, M. L., Holtom, B. C., & Pierotti, A. J. (2013). Even the best laid plans sometimes go askew: Career self-management processes, career shocks, and the decision to pursue graduate education. Journal of Applied Psychology, 98(1), 169–182. https://doi.org/10.1037/a0030882.

Shelton, C.H. (2022, August 29). 8 Ways to Avoid Quiet Quitting on Your Team. *Entrepreneur.* https://www.entrepreneur.com/leadership/8-ways-to-avoid-your-employees-quiet-quitting-on-you/434162

Simosi, M., Rousseau, D., and Daskalaki, M. (2015). When career paths cease to exist: A qualitative study of career behavior in a crisis economy. Journal of Vocational Behavior, 91, 134–146. doi.org/10.1016/j.jvb.2015.09.009

Souders, B. (2019, February 11). Flow at Work: How to Boost Engagement in the Workplace. *Positive Psychology.com.* https://positivepsychology.com/flow-at-work/

Spreitzer, G. M., Cameron, L., & Garrett, L. (2017). Alternative work arrangements: Two images of the new world of work. Annual Review of Organizational Psychology and Organizational Behavior, 4, 473–499.

Spurk, D., & Straub, C. (2020). Flexible employment relationships and careers in times of the COVID-19 pandemic. Journal of Vocational Behavior, 119.

Tenney, M. (2021). The 7 Factors of Employee Engagement. *Business Leadership Today.* https://businessleadershiptoday.com/the-7-factors-of-employee-engagement/

Thapa, A. (2022, September 2). How 'quiet quitting' became the next phase of the Great Resignation. CNBC. https://www.cnbc.com/2022/09/02/how-quiet-quitting-became-the-next-phase-of-the-great-resignation.html

The Economist (2020). Covid-19 is foisting changes on business that could be beneficial. Retrieved 18-04-2020 from: https://www.

economist.com/business/2020/03/05/covid-19-is-foisting-changes-on-business-that-could-be-beneficial.

The Great Resignation is not over: A fifth of workers plan to quit in 2022. (2022, June, 24). World Economic Forum. https://www.weforum.org/agenda/2022/06/the-great-resignation-is-not-over/

Wanberg, C. R. (2012). The individual experience of unemployment. Annual Review of Psychology, 63, 369–396.

White, B. (1995), "The career development of successful women", Women in Management Review, Vol. 10 No. 3, pp. 4-15.

World Health Organization (2020). World Health Organization Coronavirus Update. Retrieved May 5, 2020 from: https://www.who.int/emergencies/diseases/novelcoronavirus-2019.

World Health Organization (2020). World Health Organization Coronavirus Update. Retrieved May 5, 2020 from: https://www.who.int/emergencies/diseases/novelcoronavirus-2019.

Yoon, H. J., Chang, Y. C., Sadique, F., and Al Balushi, I. (2021). Mechanisms for Hopeful Employee Career Development in COVID-19: A Hope-Action Theory Perspective. Advances in Developing Human Resources 2021, Vol. 23(3) 203–221

Zenger, J, & Folkman, J. (2022, August 31). Quiet Quitting Is About Bad Bosses, Not Bad Employees. *Harvard Business Review.* https://hbr.org/2022/08/quiet-quitting-is-about-bad-bosses-not-bad-employees

INDEX

Previous book by the Author:

Published by:
AuthorHouse™
1663 Liberty Drive
Bloomington, IN 47403
www.authorhouse.com

ABOUT THE AUTHOR

Adebayo Akinloye is a global talent-succession professional with over two decades of HR practice and consulting experience. He specialises in all phases of strong internal talent benchstrength and organisational development strategy—identifying employee development gaps, identifying talent-succession needs and goals, metrics, processes and tools, training and development to build internal capacity, creating talent-succession communication plans for business leaders, facilitating talent review meetings, coaching others  for performance, creating high potential and leadership development programmes, designing assessment and development centre, competency framework and performance management, and graduate development programme to meet specific organisational needs. He leads the discussion, diagnosis, recommendation, and delivery of solutions across the talent management value chain.

His experience cuts across the information technology, telecommunications, oil and gas, automotive, earth-moving equipment and heavy machineries, pharmaceutical and manufacturing sectors. Over the years, he has established himself as a highly skilled professional of repute. An associate member of CIPD, UK and member CIPM, Nigeria. Akinloye is an accredited user of a host of global talent assessment and development tools. He has significant experience in the development and provisioning of assessment services while working with HR, Business Leaders, and Industrial Psychologists in the area of individual assessment and development.

Akinloye has handled various talent-succession and organisational development projects across different industries and countries. His professional experience cuts across multi-national, private, and successful family-owned businesses including, May & Baker Nigeria Plc, MTN Nigeria, DAL Group of Companies, North Africa, and as Group Head of HR in Century Group.

Akinloye is a graduate of Management Sciences from the University of Jos, Nigeria, with a diploma in HR Management from Cornell University, USA, and a master's degree in International Human Resource Management from Cranfield University School of Management, UK. He also holds a post-graduate diploma in "Psychology of Work" from University of Leicester, United Kingdom.

Contact Akinloye via: asa@talentsuccession.com or call: +2348032009413

www.ingramcontent.com/pod-product-compliance
Lightning Source LLC
Chambersburg PA
CBHW021437210526
45463CB00002B/553